Microsoft Azure IaaS Essentials

Design, configure, and build your cloud-based
infrastructure using Microsoft Azure

Gethyn Ellis

BIRMINGHAM - MUMBAI

Microsoft Azure IaaS Essentials

First published: May 2015

Production reference: 1260515

Published by Packt Publishing Ltd.
Livery Place
35 Livery Street
Birmingham B3 2PB, UK.

ISBN 978-1-78217-463-9

www.packtpub.com

Credits

Author
Gethyn Ellis

Reviewers
Ken Cenerelli
Yatish Patil

Commissioning Editor
Amarabha Banerjee

Acquisition Editor
Harsha Bharwani

Content Development Editor
Gaurav Sharma

Technical Editors
Dhiraj Chandanshive
Taabish Khan

Copy Editor
Rashmi Sawant

Project Coordinator
Bijal Patel

Proofreaders
Stephen Copestake
Safis Editing

Indexer
Hemangini Bari

Production Coordinator
Nitesh Thakur

Cover Work
Nitesh Thakur

About the Author

Gethyn Ellis runs a small IT consulting and training company that offers services to cloud, virtualization, and database technologies. He is based mainly in the UK and has been working with clients in both the private and public sectors. He does, however, support clients in both North America and the rest of Europe. He has been involved in several projects in deploying a virtual machine infrastructure to Azure and other cloud offerings. He has also written *Getting Started with SQL Server 2014 Administration*, *Packt Publishing*. You can follow his blog at http://www.gethynellis.com.

I would like to mention my mum and dad, Lynda and Ron Ellis, for encouraging me to write this book. I would also like to mention my two golden retriever dogs, Seth and Jake, who helped me dearly during the writing of this book by providing the necessary distractions from the writing process by demanding regular long walks.

About the Reviewers

Ken Cenerelli is a developer who specializes in designing and creating strong, data-driven web applications using the Microsoft .NET framework. He is also a member of the Microsoft Azure Canadian Community Experts team. Prior to his career in computers, he worked as a journalist in the newspaper industry. As a public speaker on emerging technologies, he has spoken at conferences across North America.

Ken lives in Ontario, Canada, with his wife, Renée. He blogs regularly at `https://kencenerelli.wordpress.com` and can be found on Twitter via `@KenCenerelli`.

Yatish Patil is a technology innovation and cloud consulting expert working with Saviant Consulting. His focus is to help businesses accelerate their growth using Cloud, Mobility, and Analytic, as well as Internet of Things (IoT). He is an expert in delivering enterprise application using Microsoft Azure, ASP.NET, and MVC. He has completed his certification in Developing Azure Solutions under Microsoft Azure Certification.

His specialties include technology innovations with Azure Machine Learning and IoT solutions; technological innovations with Microsoft Azure; Microsoft .NET, MVC, ASP.NET, C#, SQL Server, and SQL Azure; and Agile and Iterative (Scrum).

> I would like to thank all the people with whom I have worked, gained a lot experience, have reached this level, especially while working at Saviant Consulting. I gained a lot of knowledge I have as of now. I would expect the same support in future as well in order to continue exceeding in technology, innovation, and consulting.

www.PacktPub.com

Support files, eBooks, discount offers, and more

For support files and downloads related to your book, please visit www.PacktPub.com.

Did you know that Packt offers eBook versions of every book published, with PDF and ePub files available? You can upgrade to the eBook version at www.PacktPub.com and as a print book customer, you are entitled to a discount on the eBook copy. Get in touch with us at service@packtpub.com for more details.

At www.PacktPub.com, you can also read a collection of free technical articles, sign up for a range of free newsletters and receive exclusive discounts and offers on Packt books and eBooks.

https://www2.packtpub.com/books/subscription/packtlib

Do you need instant solutions to your IT questions? PacktLib is Packt's online digital book library. Here, you can search, access, and read Packt's entire library of books.

Why subscribe?

- Fully searchable across every book published by Packt
- Copy and paste, print, and bookmark content
- On demand and accessible via a web browser

Free access for Packt account holders

If you have an account with Packt at www.PacktPub.com, you can use this to access PacktLib today and view 9 entirely free books. Simply use your login credentials for immediate access.

Instant updates on new Packt books

Get notified! Find out when new books are published by following @PacktEnterprise on Twitter or the *Packt Enterprise* Facebook page.

Table of Contents

Preface

Cloud computing has been a buzzword in the IT industry for some time, and there are several cloud providers on the market. Microsoft Azure is Microsoft's cloud offering. Microsoft Azure has evolved very quickly over the last few years and now offers a comprehensive set of services, including Infrastructure as a Service (IaaS). In this book, we will start by explaining what is meant by some cloud terminology. We will take a look at how we can deploy both Windows/Linux-based virtual machines in Azure. We will take a look at how to set up a virtual network, so that our cloud-based resources can communicate with each other. Much like an on-premises server, our cloud-based servers will need to be monitored for any potential issues, and we will take a look at how we can design cloud systems that are both highly available and fault-tolerant.

What this book covers

Chapter 1, Introduction to Microsoft Azure Cloud Services, discusses some of the terminology around cloud, from the services offered to some of the specific features available in Microsoft Azure. You should be able to differentiate between a public and private cloud.

Chapter 2, Creating and Deploying a Windows Virtual Machine, shows you how we can create a new Windows-based virtual machine in Microsoft Azure. We will take a look at how we can connect to and work on the virtual machine and how we can control the VM using PowerShell. Finally, we will see how we can convert an existing server and make it an Azure-based VM.

Chapter 3, Deploying Linux Virtual Machines on Azure, shows you how we can create and configure a Linux-based virtual machine in Microsoft Azure's cloud. We will take a look at the different flavors of Linux available, how we can create the virtual machine, how we can use the command-line interface and Putty, and how we can connect via RDP to work with Linux.

Chapter 4, *Virtual Networks*, shows you how we can create a virtual network in Azure. We will take a look at how we can approach moving an existing virtual machine to a new virtual network and what is needed to configure point-to-site connectivity for hybrid networks that allow you to combine your on-premises network with your cloud-based resources.

Chapter 5, *Managing and Monitoring Virtual Machines*, shows you how we can set up and collect the diagnostic information on our cloud-based virtual machine. We will take a look at what we need to do in order to store this information in the cloud and also how we can integrate the monitoring with on-premises tools, such as SCOM.

Chapter 6, *Microsoft Azure and Active Directory*, discusses the options that are available to you when it comes to making use of Microsoft Azure Directory Services. We will take a look at how we can create a cloud-based directory and discuss the options available for integrating your on-premises Active Directory with the cloud.

Chapter 7, *High Availability and Disaster Recovery for Azure Virtual Machines*, shows you the High Availability options that you have when configuring virtual machines in Azure. You have a number of options available to you when you configure both your Azure-based VMs to be highly available, including the ability to create availability sets. You can make use of site recovery to use the Azure cloud as a disaster recovery site for both your cloud-based virtual machines and on-premises Hyper-V virtual machines.

What you need for this book

All you need for this book is a subscription to Microsoft Azure. In this case, it's perfectly acceptable to use the free trial subscription.

Who this book is for

This book is for system administrators and developers who want to get an understanding of how to deploy virtual machines to the cloud.

Conventions

In this book, you will find a number of text styles that distinguish between different kinds of information. Here are some examples of these styles and an explanation of their meaning.

Code words in text, database table names, folder names, filenames, file extensions, pathnames, dummy URLs, user input, and Twitter handles are shown as follows: "Then, you are ready to upload your .vhd file."

A block of code is set as follows:

```
New-AzureAlert `
    -alertName "High CPU" `
    -alertDescription "Higher than 85% CPU utilization" `
    -subscriptionId $subscriptionId `
```

Any command-line input or output is written as follows:

```
Add-AzureVhd -Destination "<BlobStorageURL>/<vhdimage>/<VHDName>.vhd"
-LocalFilePath <PathToVHDFile>
```

New terms and **important words** are shown in bold. Words that you see on the screen, for example, in menus or dialog boxes, appear in the text like this: "Click on the **Create Storage Account** button to create the storage account."

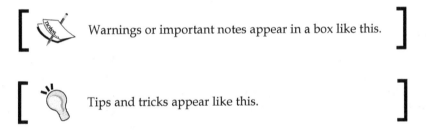

Warnings or important notes appear in a box like this.

Tips and tricks appear like this.

Reader feedback

Feedback from our readers is always welcome. Let us know what you think about this book—what you liked or disliked. Reader feedback is important for us as it helps us develop titles that you will really get the most out of.

To send us general feedback, simply e-mail feedback@packtpub.com, and mention the book's title in the subject of your message.

If there is a topic that you have expertise in and you are interested in either writing or contributing to a book, see our author guide at www.packtpub.com/authors.

Customer support

Now that you are the proud owner of a Packt book, we have a number of things to help you to get the most from your purchase.

Downloading the example code

You can download the example code files from your account at `http://www.packtpub.com` for all the Packt Publishing books you have purchased. If you purchased this book elsewhere, you can visit `http://www.packtpub.com/support` and register to have the files e-mailed directly to you.

Downloading the color images of this book

We also provide you with a PDF file that has color images of the screenshots/diagrams used in this book. The color images will help you better understand the changes in the output. You can download this file from `http://www.packtpub.com/sites/default/files/downloads/1234OT_ColorImages.pdf`.

Errata

Although we have taken every care to ensure the accuracy of our content, mistakes do happen. If you find a mistake in one of our books — maybe a mistake in the text or the code — we would be grateful if you could report this to us. By doing so, you can save other readers from frustration and help us improve subsequent versions of this book. If you find any errata, please report them by visiting `http://www.packtpub.com/submit-errata`, selecting your book, clicking on the **Errata Submission Form** link, and entering the details of your errata. Once your errata are verified, your submission will be accepted and the errata will be uploaded to our website or added to any list of existing errata under the Errata section of that title.

To view the previously submitted errata, go to `https://www.packtpub.com/books/content/support` and enter the name of the book in the search field. The required information will appear under the **Errata** section.

Piracy

Piracy of copyrighted material on the Internet is an ongoing problem across all media. At Packt, we take the protection of our copyright and licenses very seriously. If you come across any illegal copies of our works in any form on the Internet, please provide us with the location address or website name immediately so that we can pursue a remedy.

Please contact us at copyright@packtpub.com with a link to the suspected pirated material.

We appreciate your help in protecting our authors and our ability to bring you valuable content.

Questions

If you have a problem with any aspect of this book, you can contact us at questions@packtpub.com, and we will do our best to address the problem.

1
Introduction to Microsoft Azure Cloud Services

Cloud is a buzzword that has been bandied about the technology industry for the last few years, but what exactly does this mean. What does cloud mean for the people working in IT departments around the world? How will cloud affect the way you do your job, how you work, and what type of work you do? I guess these are questions that are yet to be answered fully, but in this book, we will try and give some meaning to the term cloud from a technology perspective, and then we will spend some time to take a look at the Microsoft's Azure cloud offering, and discuss some of the services you can get from Microsoft's cloud.

This chapter is intended to provide a grounding in some of the terminology associated with cloud computing, and then we will take a look at what we need to do in order to be able to work with Microsoft Azure and the services that Microsoft offers through this platform.

In this chapter, you will learn the following topics:

- A definition of cloud computing
- Cloud services terminology
- An introduction to Microsoft Azure

Understanding cloud computing

What do we mean when we talk about cloud from an information technology perspective? People mention cloud services; where do we get the services from? What services are offered?

The Wikipedia definition of cloud computing is as follows:

> *"Cloud computing is a computing term or metaphor that evolved in the late 1990s, based on utility and consumption of computer resources. Cloud computing involves application systems which are executed within the cloud and operated through internet enabled devices. Purely cloud computing does not rely on the use of cloud storage as it will be removed upon users download action. Clouds can be classified as public, private and [hybrid cloud | hybrid]."*

If you have worked with virtualization, then the concept of cloud is not completely alien to you. With virtualization, you can group a bunch of powerful hardware together, using a hypervisor. A hypervisor is a kind of software, operating system, or firmware that allows you to run virtual machines. Some of the popular Hypervisors on the market are VMware ESX or Microsoft's Hyper-V. Then, you can use this powerful hardware to run a set of virtual servers or guests. The guests share the resources of the host in order to execute and provide the services and computing resources of your IT department. The IT department takes care of everything from maintaining the hypervisor hosts to managing and maintaining the virtual servers and guests. The internal IT department does all the work. This is sometimes termed as a private cloud.

Third-party suppliers, such as Microsoft, VMware, and Amazon, have a public cloud offering. With a public cloud, some computing services are provided to you on the Internet, and you can pay for what you use, which is like a utility bill. For example, let's take the utilities you use at home. This model can be really useful for start-up business that might not have an accurate demand forecast for their services, or the demand may change very quickly. Cloud computing can also be very useful for established businesses, who would like to make use of the elastic billing model. The more services you consume, the more you pay when you get billed at the end of the month. There are various types of public cloud offerings and services from a number of different providers. The TechNet top ten cloud providers are as follows:

1. VMware
2. Microsoft
3. Bluelock
4. Citrix
5. Joyent
6. Terrmark
7. Salesforce.com

8. Century Link
9. RackSpace
10. Amazon Web Services

It is interesting to read that in 2013, Microsoft was only listed ninth in the list. With a new CEO, Microsoft has taken a new direction and put its Azure cloud offering at the heart of the business model. To quote one TechNet 2014 attendee:

> *"TechNet this year was all about Azure, even the on premises stuff was built on the Azure model"*

With a different direction, it seems pretty clear that Microsoft is investing heavily in its cloud offering, and this will be further enhanced with further investment. This will allow a hybrid cloud environment, a combination of on-premises and public cloud, to be combined to offer organizations that ultimate flexibility when it comes to consuming IT resources.

Services offered

The term cloud is used to describe a variety of service offerings from multiple providers. You could argue, in fact, that the term cloud doesn't actually mean anything specific in terms of the service that you're consuming. It is, in fact, just a term that means you are consuming an IT service from a provider. Be it an internal IT department in the form of a private cloud or a public offering from some cloud provider, a public cloud, or it could be some combination of both in the form of a hybrid cloud. So, then what are the services that cloud providers offer?

Virtualization and on-premises technology

Most business even in today's cloudy environment has some on-premises technology. Until virtualization became popular and widely deployed several years ago, it was very common to have a one-to-one relationship between a physical hardware server with its own physical resources, such as CPU, RAM, storage, and the operating system installed on the physical server. It became clear that in this type of environment, you would need a lot of physical servers in your data center.

An expanding and sometimes, a sprawling environment brings its own set of problems. The servers need cooling and heat management as well as a power source, and all the hardware and software needs to be maintained. Also, in terms of utilization, this model left lots of resources under-utilized:

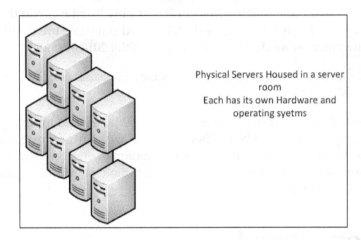

Virtualization changed this to some extent. With virtualization, you can create several guests or virtual servers that are configured to share the resources of the underlying host, each with their own operating system installed. It is possible to run both a Windows and Linux guest on the same physical host using virtualization. This allows you to maximize the resource utilization and allows your business to get a better return on investment on its hardware infrastructure:

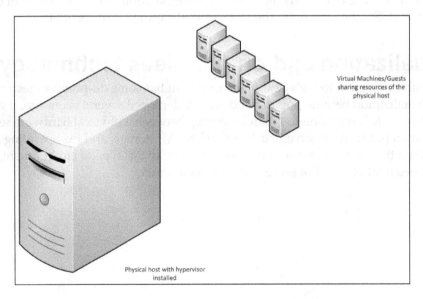

Virtualization is very much a precursor to cloud; many virtualized environments are sometimes called private clouds, so having an understanding of virtualization and how it works will give you a good grounding in some of the concepts of a cloud-based infrastructure.

Software as a service (SaaS)

SaaS is a subscription where you need to pay to use the software for the time that you're using it. You don't own any of the infrastructures, and you don't have to manage any of the servers or operating systems, you simply consume the software that you will be using. You can think of SaaS as like taking a taxi ride. When you take a taxi ride, you don't own the car, you don't need to maintain the car, and you don't even drive the car. You simply tell the taxi driver or his company when and where you want to travel somewhere, and they will take care of getting you there. The longer the trip, that is, the longer you use the taxi, the more you pay.

An example of Microsoft's Software as a service would be the Azure SQL Database. The following diagram shows the cloud-based SQL databse:

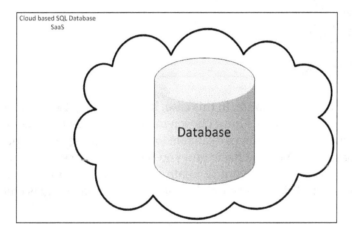

Microsoft offers customers a SQL database that is fully hosted and maintained in Microsoft data centers, and the customer simply has to make use of the service and the database. So, we can compare this to having an on-premises database. To have an on-premises database, you need a Windows Server machine (physical or virtual) with the appropriate version of SQL Server installed. The server would need enough CPU, RAM, and storage to fulfill the needs of your database, and you need to manage and maintain the environment, applying various patches to the operating systems as they become available, installing, and testing various SQL Server service packs as they become available, and all the while, your application makes use of the database platform.

With the SQL Azure database, you have no overhead, you simply need to connect to the Microsoft Azure portal and request a SQL database by following the wizard:

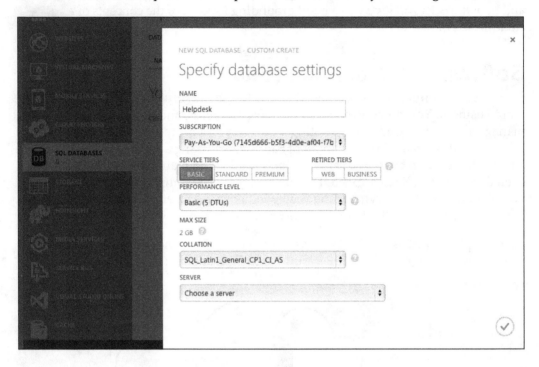

Simply, give the database a name. In this case, it's called Helpdesk, select the service tier you want. In this example, I have chosen the **Basic** service tier. The service tier will define things, such as the resources available to your database, and impose limits, in terms of database size. With the **Basic** tier, you have a database size limit of 2 GB. You can specify the server that you want to create your database with, accept the defaults on the other settings, click on the check button, and the database gets created:

It's really that simple. You will then pay for what you use in terms of database size and data access. In a later section, you will see how to set up a Microsoft Azure account.

Platform as a service (PaaS)

With PaaS, you rent the hardware, operating system, storage, and network from the public cloud service provider. PaaS is an offshoot of SaaS. Initially, SaaS didn't take off quickly, possibly because of the lack of control that IT departments and business thought they were going to suffer as a result of using the SaaS cloud offering. Going back to the transport analogy, you can compare PaaS to car rentals. When you rent a car, you don't need to make the car, you don't need to own the car, and you have no responsibility to maintain the car. You do, however, need to drive the car if you are going to get to your required destination. In PaaS terms, the developer and the system administrator have slightly more control over how the environment is set up and configured but still much of the work is taken care of by the cloud service provider. So, the hardware, operating system, and all the other components that run your application are managed and taken care of by the cloud provider, but you get a little more control over how things are configured. A geographically dispersed website would be a good example of an application offered on a PaaS offering.

Infrastructure as a service (IaaS)

With IaaS, you have much more control over the environment, and everything is customizable. Going with the transport analogy again, you can compare it to buying a car. The service provides you with the car upfront, and you are then responsible for using the car to ensure that it gets you from A to B. You are also responsible to fix the car if something goes wrong, and also ensure that the car is maintained by servicing it regularly, adding fuel, checking the tyre pressure, and so on. You have more control, but you also have more to do in terms of maintenance.

Microsoft Azure has an offering. You can deploy a virtual machine, you can specify what OS you want, how much RAM you want the virtual machine to have, you can specify where the server will sit in terms of Microsoft data centers, and you can set up and configure recoverability and high availability for your Azure virtual machine:

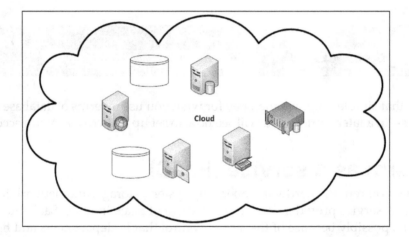

Hybrid environments

With a hybrid environment, you get a combination of on-premises infrastructure and cloud services. It allows you to flexibly add resilience and high availability to your existing infrastructure. It's perfectly possible for the cloud to act as a disaster recovery site for your existing infrastructure. In the rest of this book, we will take a look at how you can work with Microsoft Azure's cloud platform to make use of its infrastructure, as a service offering, and also how you can combine it with your own internal infrastructure to build your own hybrid environment:

Microsoft Azure

In order to work with the examples in this book, you need sign up for a Microsoft account. You can visit `http://azure.microsoft.com/`, and create an account all by yourself by completing the necessary form as follows:

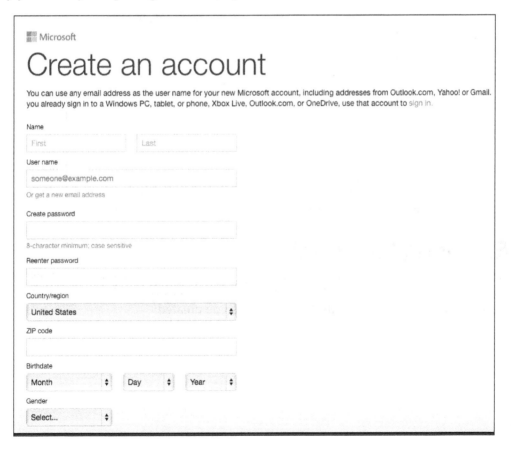

Here, you simply enter your details; you can use your e-mail address as your username. Enter the credentials specified.

Return to the Azure website, and if you want to make use of the free trial, click on the free trial link. Currently, you get $125 worth of free Azure services. Once you have clicked on the free trial link, you will have to verify your details. You will also need to enter a credit card number and its details. Microsoft assures that you won't be charged during the free trial. Enter the appropriate details and click on **Sign Up**:

Exploring the portal

Return to www.azure.microsoft.com, and you will now sign in to the portal using the credentials that you created in the previous step. Click on the **Portal** link at the top of the page, and log in with the credentials you created:

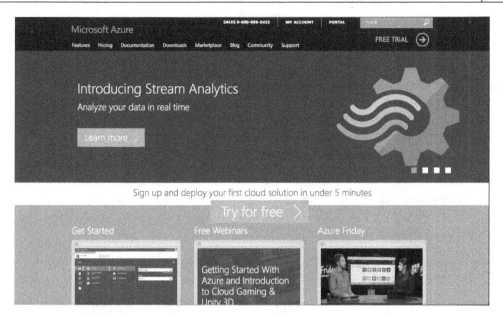

Once you have clicked on the **Portal** link, you will be prompted for your e-mail address. Enter the e-mail address that you have registered with Microsoft. You will then be prompted to enter your username and password and sign in. When you have successfully signed in, you will see the Azure portal screen. I'm on the **All Items** option, as shown in the following screenshot:

In the preceding screenshot, you can see that I have two items listed: the **Default Directory**, which is there by default, and the **Helpdesk** SQL database that I created earlier in the chapter.

Under the **All Items** option, you have the website options. This is a SaaS offering where you can create and host a new site. There are some gallery options, so you can select an off-the-shelf website if you wish. The gallery includes many different options, including CMS, e-commerce websites, forums, and wikis. In theory, you could get a pretty powerful website up and running with very little effort.

Then, you have the **Virtual Machines** option; we will take a look at this in more detail throughout the course of the book. Currently, we don't have any virtual machines created. We will discuss all the options to create Azure virtual machines in a later chapter.

Mobile services allow you to integrate your mobile applications with the cloud, including storing your data in a SQL database.

Cloud services are again used in mobile app development. To quote from the Azure website:

> *"Develop, package, and deploy powerful applications and services to the cloud with Azure Cloud Services and the click of a button. Scale from 1 to 1000 in minutes. Once your application is deployed, that's it: From provisioning, to load balancing, to health monitoring, Azure handles the rest. Your application is backed by an industry-leading 99.95% monthly SLA."*

Next, we have the SQL databases; again, this is a SaaS offering. If you want to create a SQL database, you can simply click on the **create database** option. Give your database a name. I'll call mine DogsPantry, and select the subscription you want to use to pay for the databases. In your case, you will be using the free trial subscription that we created earlier. You then need to choose a service tier. This defines the limits that are imposed on your database in terms of performance. Unsurprisingly, here, the more performance you want, the more it will cost. There are three service tiers:

- **Basic**
- **Standard**
- **Premium**

Performance is measured in database throughput units (DTUs). These units provide a way to describe how the performance differs between the tiers:

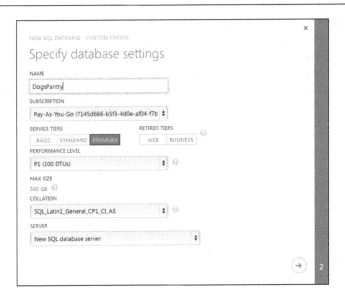

DTUs are a measure of CPU, memory, reads, and writes. In theory SQL code aside, the more DTUs you have, the more performance you get. With the **Basic** tier, you get five DTUs and a database size limit of 2 GB. The **Sandard** tier offers three levels within it: S0, S1, and S2; as the number increases, so does the DTUs and hence, the performance you get. The **Premium** tier also offers three levels: P1, P2 and P3. The P3 Premium level offers 800 DTUs, which, in theory, should offer you 160 times the performance compared to **Basic** and also allows you to have a database of up to 500 GB in size. This is 250 times the size of the maximum database in the **Basic** tier.

Then, you can choose the collation that you want and a new server for it to be deployed to. Then, you can specify a login ID and password, and there, you have your brandspanking new cloud-based database:

The next option in the portal is **Storage**. This is where you can create a cloud-based storage service for your elastic storage needs. Azure virtual machines make use of Azure storage, so we will take a look at this feature in more detail in the upcoming chapters. This storage can also be useful, for example, with SQL Server 2014, you can back up your database to Azure storage. This is where it stores your backup file.

HDInsight is Microsoft's cloud-based Hadoop offering:

This is cloud-based big data. To quote from the Azure website:

> *"HDInsight is a Hadoop distribution powered by the cloud. This means HDInsight was architected to handle any amount of data, scaling from terabytes to petabytes on demand. You can spin up any number of nodes at anytime. We charge only for the compute and storage you actually use."*

We won't be looking at this option in any detail in this book, but if you are working with the cloud and big data, this might be an option that might interest you. You also have the ability to work with machine learning and streaming analytics.

Next, we have the **Media Services** option that allow you to stream video to a range of devices, and we also have the service bus, which is a cloud-based messaging system:

It can be used to connect just about anything. You can use it to connect on-premises technology to cloud-based resources. You can even use it to connect household appliances, such as your central heating system, to a device, such as a tablet or iPad.

Visual Studio Online is exactly what it says; Microsoft's online offering of Visual Studio. Then, we have Cache Services and BizTalk. The following quote describes what the caching services offer:

> *"Azure Managed Cache Service provides a way for you to perform caching that helps you build fast, scalable applications in Microsoft Azure through a secure, dedicated cache. A secure, dedicated cache is created for you in the region of your choice and you have total control over the cache, guaranteeing isolation of your business critical data."*

We will take a look at **Recovery Services** in more detail in *Chapter 7, High Availability and Disaster Recovery for Azure Virtual Machines*. However, this is the option we will use for site recovery services and backups, and this will play an important role in implementing a robust backup and recovery plan.

The **Scheduler** option will be used as a scheduling tool and is ideal for automating certain tasks to run at a specific time. This can include things, such as backup jobs, which we will discuss in *Chapter 7, High Availability and Disaster Recovery for Azure Virtual Machines*. The ability to create a virtual network allows you to expand your on-premises data center to the cloud, building hybrid IT environments and business applications.

Management services will be used to manage and monitor the cloud environment and the Azure-based Active Directory that can be integrated with your on-premises Windows Active Directory.

Summary

In this chapter, we looked at and discussed some of the terminology around the cloud. From the services offered to some of the specific features available in Microsoft Azure, you should be able to differentiate between a public and private cloud. You can also now differentiate between some of the public cloud offerings. Then, at the end of this chapter, we looked at some of the specific Microsoft Azure features and services.

In the next set of chapters, we will take a look specifically at how we can make use of some of these infrastructures and platforms as service offerings.

2
Creating and Deploying a Windows Virtual Machine

In this chapter, we will focus on deploying a virtual machine to Microsoft Azure. In this chapter, you will learn the following topics:

- Creating a new virtual machine running Windows
- Connecting to your Windows virtual machine
- Deploying an existing Windows server to Azure

In this chapter, we will deploy a virtual machine with a Windows server installed. We will take a look at the options to connect to the virtual machine and then, we will discuss the options to deploy an existing server, either a physical or virtual server, to Microsoft Azure.

Creating a new Windows server virtual machine

In order to create a new virtual machine in Microsoft Azure, you need to have a Microsoft Azure account. This was discussed in *Chapter 1, Introduction to Microsoft Azure Cloud Services*. Feel free to revert if you need any guidance on creating your Microsoft Azure account. If you have already created your Microsoft Azure account, visit https://azure.microsoft.com.

Now, to start with, let's take a look at the following procedures:

1. Log in to the portal using the link on the home screen:

2. Click on the **Portal** link, and log in with the e-mail address that you registered with Microsoft Azure in *Chapter 1, Introduction to Microsoft Azure Cloud Services*.

3. If you have already signed in using your computer, your browser and the Azure web page may already recognize you. You can log in by clicking on the e-mail address that is being displayed:

4. I was able to log in to the portal by clicking on my e-mail address. If a wrong e-mail address is being displayed, then you can click on the **Use another account** option:

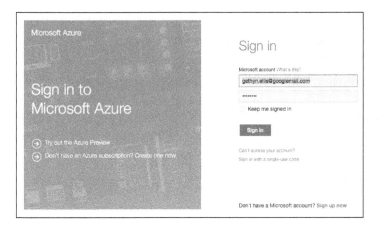

5. You will be prompted to enter your password; do so and click on **Sign in**, which should take you to the Microsoft Azure portal:

Now you are successfully logged into the portal; you can create a Windows virtual machine. We will take a look at the following two options to create a server from scratch:

1. On the left-hand side menu bar, click on the **Virtual Machines** link.

2. Click on the **Create A Virtual Machine** link in the detail pane on the right-hand side of the page.

   Notice that by default we are on the **Instances** tab in the detail pane. This is used to create a new virtual machine from scratch. The other two options, **Images** and **Disks**, will be used when we have an existing server that we want to deploy to Azure. We will take a look at these options later in this chapter:

3. Once you have clicked on the **Create A Virtual Machine** option, you will notice that the **Create New Virtual Machine** option has partly filled some of the **Create New Wizard** option. The **Compute** and **Virtual Machine** options are automatically selected:

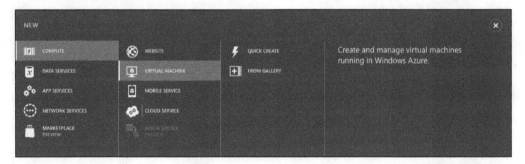

We then have the two **Quick Create** and **From Gallery** options available to use. We will create two new virtual machines using each of these options:

1. Click on **Quick Create**, and we will get an additional form to complete:

2. You need to give the virtual machine a DNS name. I have named my server `gethynellisWS`, where the WS stands for Windows server.

3. Then, we need to select an image to deploy. If we click on the drop-down list, next to the **Image** textbox, you will see the following options, as shown in the following screenshot:

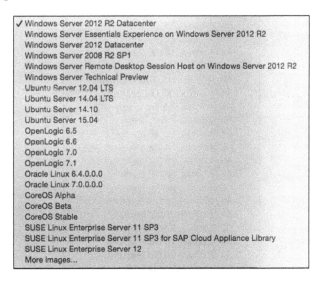

Notice that although the Windows server options are listed first, you don't have to deploy just Windows-based virtual machines to Microsoft Azure. There are images for various Linux distributions and other operating systems that can be deployed. In this case, I will select **Windows Server 2012 R2 Datacenter**.

Pricing for virtual machines

The next option that we need to pick is very important, as the size and specification we choose will define the performance that we get and also the price and cost of the virtual machine when it's running. I think you'll agree that getting this right is probably important. You can get up-to-date price information from the Microsoft Azure website (`http://azure.microsoft.com/pricing/`).

Now, the virtual machine gets billed on a per minute basis, while the machine is running. Virtual machines are supported by Microsoft Azure in both the **Basic** and **Standard** tiers along with the **Premium** tier. As I mentioned earlier, there is a hierarchical structure to the pricing. The more basic the tier, the cheaper the virtual machine is to run.

It is important to note that you only get billed when your virtual machines are running. If you have a virtual machine built but it is shut down, then the subscription will remain active, but you will not be charged. You can leave your virtual machine housed on Azure with no cost as long as it's shut down.

If you click on the drop-down list, next to **Size**, you will see a lot of options. The drop-down list looks like the following screenshot:

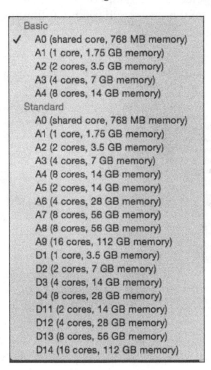

For the purposes of this demonstration, I have selected **A0** under the **Basic** tier—the cheapest option. At the time of writing, **A0** in the **Basic** tier offers the following:

- **Instance**: A0
- **Cores**: 1
- **RAM**: 0.75 GB
- **Disk Size**: 20 GB
- **Price**: £0.011 per hour (approximately £8 a month)

For comparison, the maximum size in the **Basic** tier offers the following options:

- **Instance**: D14
- **Cores**: 16
- **RAM**: 112 GB
- **Disk Size**: 800 GB
- **Price**: £1.6617 per hour (approximately £1187 a month)

As you can see, there is quite a significant difference in price, capacity, and performance. Azure pricing changes very regularly; you can check out the Azure pricing web page for the latest price information at `http://azure. microsoft.com/en-gb/pricing/`.

The **Basic** tier is perfectly fine to use for development and test purposes, so I have chosen the cheapest option for my virtual machine. You will obviously make your decision based on the performance and capacity you need and what the virtual machine will eventually be used for.

The Microsoft Azure pricing is fairly fluid; I don't want to include pricing or prices in this book, as obviously, they could change over time. For a detailed breakdown on the pricing of Microsoft Azure virtual machines, you can visit `http://azure. microsoft.com/en-us/pricing/details/virtual-machines/`.

Then, we need to create a username, which will act as the administrator on this virtual machine. For the purposes of this example, I will use `GethynEllis` as a password. You can use whatever best suits your needs here.

When it comes to the **Region/Affinity Group** section, for the purposes of this chapter, you will pick the region closest to you. I'll talk more about this option in a later chapter, which is based on networking. When the virtual machine is created, the Blob storage is used to store the image. When you choose an affinity group or a region, this can affect where, in the world, the virtual machine gets placed in the Blob storage. If you don't specify an affinity group, a Blob storage container will automatically get created in the region specified, so choose appropriately.

When complete, the page in the portal will look something like this:

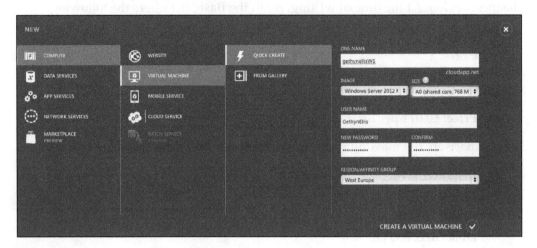

Click on the **Create A Virtual Machine** link, and the virtual machine will get created. Note that this process can take a while to complete:

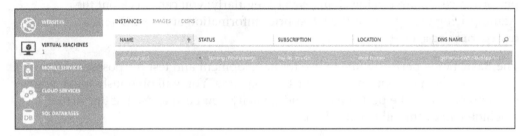

The machine will get provisioned and it will then start. When I did this, the process took over 20 minutes to complete:

Creating a virtual machine using the gallery

Depending on what you want to use the virtual machine for, you can create a virtual machine using a preconfigured image from the Microsoft Azure gallery. So, let's say we want to deploy a Windows server with a SQL Server installed, then we can use the **Gallery** option:

1. To do this, you need to be logged into the Microsoft Azure portal. Click on the **Virtual Machine** option on the left-hand side of the menu. I have already created a virtual machine and it's running. To create a new virtual machine, you need to click on the **New** button at the bottom of the page:

2. This will start the **Create Virtual Machine** wizard and again, this will be prepopulated with initial choices for a virtual machine, namely, **Compute** and **Virtual Machine**. This time, we will choose the **From Gallery** option:

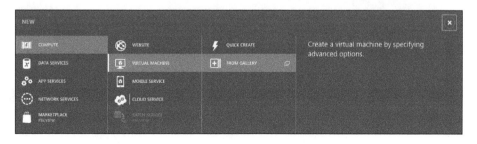

3. When you click on the **From Gallery** option, you will have a list of images that you can install. You will make a note here that there are not just Microsoft products built as images but a whole host of other products as well. As we want to deploy a SQL Server, we will select **SQL Server** from the **Microsoft** tab. You will see the list of images that can be used to provision your virtual machine:

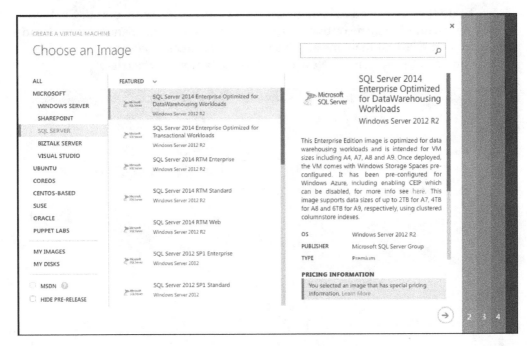

4. In this case, I am going to choose a SQL Server 2014 Standard Edition on Windows Server 2012 R2. Here, there are a whole bunch of images for SQL Server and Windows to the 2008 R2 versions of each product. I want the latest and greatest version here, but you may need an older version of the server operating system or a SQL server. Once you have chosen your image, click on the right arrow to go to the **Virtual machine configuration** screen:

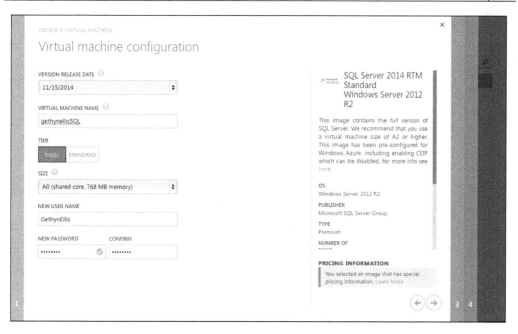

5. Here, you get to choose the version release date of your image. As cumulative updates and security patches get released, the image may change but the version of the software will not. I have chosen the latest version of the image.

6. You have to give your virtual machine a name; in this case, I have named mine `gethynellisSQL`, allowing me to identify what the virtual machine is doing and the role it is playing in my infrastructure. I have chosen the **Basic** tier here. We discussed the tiers and the size options earlier in the chapter. I have chosen **Basic** and **A0** for the purpose of this demonstration. Just to mention here, the pricing structure for a virtual machine with the SQL Server installed is higher than the prices quoted earlier in the chapter; this is due to the extra SQL Server license. In reality, you would want your SQL Server to have much more capacity than this, and Microsoft recommends that you have at least Standard A2 for your SQL Server. For this test purpose, basic **A0** is fine for my needs. Your needs will vary, and you will need to consider the capacity and performance needs when deploying to production.

7. You will need to create an administrator account. I have named mine
   `GethynEllis` with a password. Once I have confirmed the password,
   I can click on the right arrow:

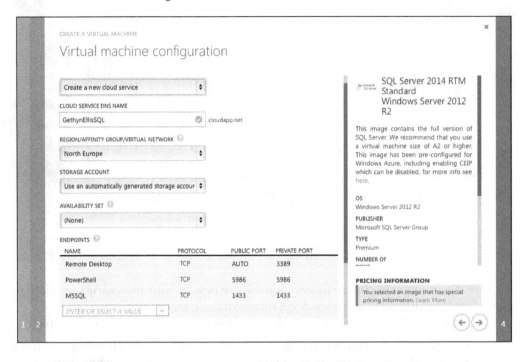

8. We will revisit some of the options here when we take a look at networking,
   high availability, load balancing, and Active Directory in later chapters, but
   for now, I am going to accept the defaults, with one exception.

9. I would like to draw your attention to the last section titled **Endpoints**.
   There will be two endpoints listed here by default, **Remote Desktop** and
   PowerShell. As this server will also act as a SQL Server, we will add the SQL
   Server endpoint here. Click on the drop-down list and scroll down until you
   see the **MSSQL** option. Select it and leave the default settings as they are and
   click on the right arrow.

10. The final screen provides you with a list of other services that can be
    configured. I am going to accept the defaults here, which will just install the
    virtual machine agent, click on the tick icon to create the new SQL Server
    virtual machine:

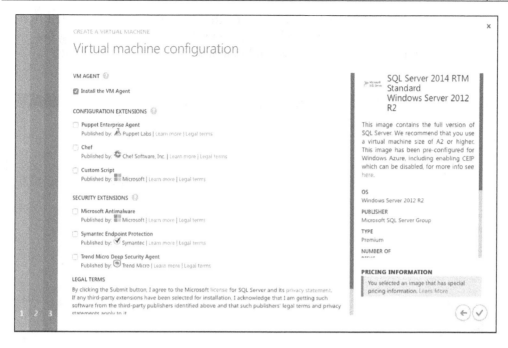

Again, this process can take some time while the virtual machine is provisioned.

Connecting and managing your new Windows server virtual machine

In this section, we will take a look at how you can connect and manage your new Windows-based virtual machine. You will learn how to start and stop and your virtual machine in the Azure portal and how you can connect to the virtual machine to work on it.

Starting and stopping the virtual machine

You can start and stop your virtual machine using the Microsoft Azure portal as follows:

1. To start and stop the virtual machine, you need to be logged into the Azure portal.

2. When you are logged into the portal, you need to select the **Virtual Machines** option on the left-hand side of the page.

3. In the following screenshot, you can see that, currently, I have created two virtual machines and they are both running. The process of creating the virtual machine will start the virtual machine, so both of my virtual machines are currently running:

4. To stop or power off the virtual machine, we will use the menu footer toolbar:

5. Click on the **Shut Down** button. You will receive a warning that the IP address currently allocated to the virtual machine will be released.

6. You need to click on **Yes**, and the machine will shut down. This process can take some time, so be patient while the virtual machine powers itself off:

When the virtual machine has powered off, the menu options in the footer menu bar will change. We will now have the option in this menu bar to start the virtual machine.

7. Click on the start button to boot up the virtual machine.

In the last section, we discussed the process of powering on and booting up your virtual machines. We also looked at how to power off and shut down your virtual machines. You would want to power off all the machines that you are not using to save on cost.

Connecting to a virtual machine in the portal

When you have your virtual machines powered up, you will likely want to connect to them so that you can work with them and configure them to work with your applications. To connect to your virtual machine, there is a connect option in the **Portal Footer** menu. Ensure that the virtual machine you want to **Connect** to is selected and click on **Connect**.

You will be prompted to download an .rdp file. This will download an .rdp file that will allow you to connect via the Remote Desktop Protocol (RDP). Click on **OK** to download the file:

Connecting from the Remote Desktop Protocol (RDP)

When you have downloaded the .rdp file, go to the downloads folder on your computer. The location of this file will depend on which browser you are using to access Azure. Double-click on the downloaded .rdp file. As I'm trying to connect to GethynellisSQL, I have a GethynEllisSQL.rdp file.

I'll double-click on this file, and this will open up an RDP session. I am using Mac to connect, so I need to have a Mac RDP software to run Mac. You can see that it has prepopulated the server name with the full address of my `GethynellisSQL` server:

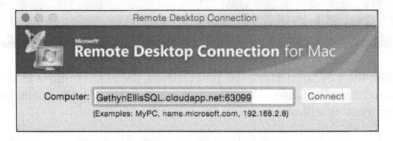

Click on **Connect** and enter the administrator username and password that we created during the virtual machine setup, and you will be able to connect to your virtual machine. You will be logged into the Windows console:

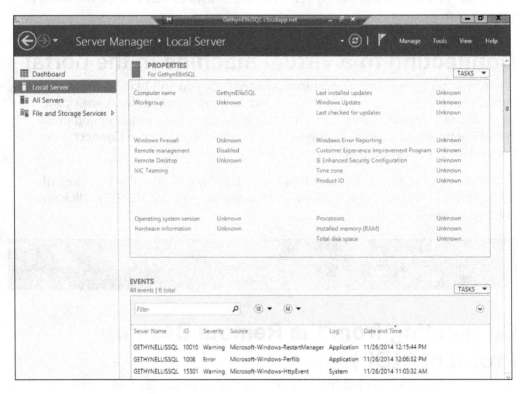

You can then work with your Azure-based cloud virtual machine like you would with any other server.

Working with your virtual machine with PowerShell

When we created the two virtual machines earlier in this chapter, the RDP and PowerShell endpoints were installed by default. PowerShell has become Microsoft's scripting language of choice over the last few years. You can use PowerShell to work with and manage your Azure-based virtual machines. You will need PowerShell for Azure, which you can download and install from `http://azure.microsoft.com/en-gb/documentation/articles/install-configure-powershell/#Install`.

Follow the installation wizard, and when you have Azure PowerShell installed, you can connect to your Microsoft Azure account. I'm using Windows 7, so I can start Azure PowerShell by navigating to **Start** | **All Programs** | **Microsoft Azure PowerShell**. This will take you to the Microsoft Azure PowerShell command line:

1. On the command prompt, you can type the following command:

    Add-azureaccount

2. Press **Enter**:

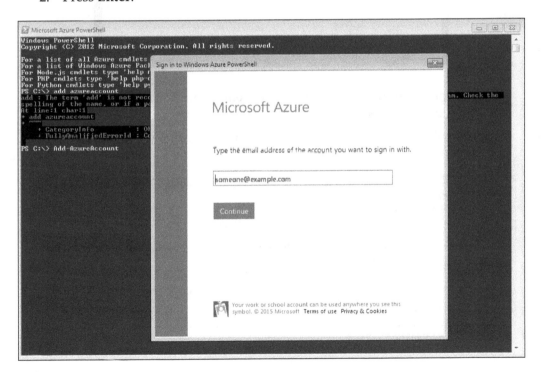

3. You will be prompted to sign in with your Microsoft Azure account:

4. Click on **Continue**. If prompted, please enter your Microsoft Azure password on the next screen, and click on **Sign In**.

You will get a confirmation on the command line that your account has been registered:

5. You can list the accounts added by running the following command:

   ```
   Get-AzureAccount
   ```

   This will list the accounts that have been registered with Azure PowerShell.

6. You can get a list of the virtual machines that are associated with your Microsoft Azure account by running the following command:

   ```
   Get-AzureVM
   ```

   You can see that we have two virtual machines listed.

   You can start, stop, and restart the virtual machines using PowerShell too.

7. To stop the virtual server called `Gethynellis WS`, run the following command:

   ```
   Stop-AzureVM -ServiceName "gethynellisWS" -Name
   "gethynellisWS" -StayProvisoned
   ```

8. To start the virtual machine again, you can run the following the command:

   ```
   Start-AzureVM -ServiceName "gethynellisWS" -
   Name"gethynellisWS"
   ```

   This will start the virtual machine.

Adding additional data disks to your virtual machine

You may want or need to increase the storage capacity of your virtual machine. In order to achieve this, you may want to add extra data disks to your virtual server. We will use the Azure portal to do this. Ensure that you are logged in, and you have selected the **Virtual Machine** option on the left-hand side menu.

Select the virtual machine where you want to add the disks. In this case, I will add the disk to the `GethynEllisSQL` virtual machine. Ensure that the virtual machine is highlighted, and in the footer options menu, choose **Attach** and click on **Empty Disk**:

Then, we will need to complete the new disk wizard. You need to complete the **Attach an empty disk to the virtual machine** wizard:

Follow these steps to add additional disks to your virtual machine:

1. I am accepting the default options for the virtual machine and the storage location. I will name the file `SQLServerData` and a VHD will be created. I have set the file to `10` GB in size. I am going to leave the host cache preference as **None**, which is the default value. Then, click on the tick icon to create the disk. You can then click on the **Storage** option on the left-hand side menu bar, and click on the location that was specified for your disk. You will see that a new VHD has been created:

2. The next thing that we need to do is present the VHD to the server and mount it on a drive letter. To do this, I will connect to the `GethynEllisSQL` server via RDP.

3. Once you have logged into the server, you will use Server Manager to present the drive to Windows. Click on the **Server Manager** button, which can be found at the bottom of the menu bar, of the virtual machine When the Server Manager starts, click on the **Files and Storage Services** option on the left-hand side menu. Once this page loads, click on the **Disk** option on the left-hand side menu of **Files and Storage Services**.

4. You will see the disk that we created earlier listed in the list of disks:

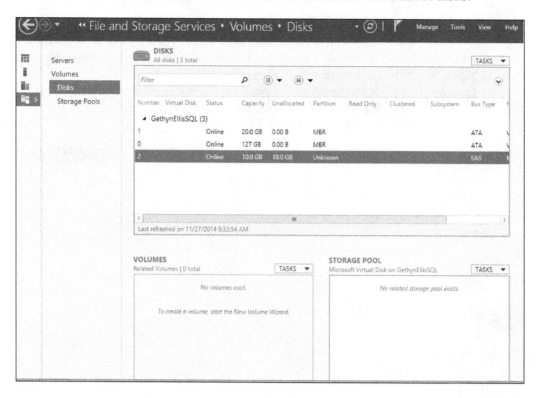

5. Right-click on the disk we just created; in this case, it's disk 2 and choose **New Volume**.

6. This will bring us to the **New Volume Wizard**. The first page describes what the wizard does; you can read that if you wish. Then, click on **Next**.

7. On the next screen, you need to choose the server that the disk is going to be provisioned to. In this case, only GethynEllisSQL is present and this is the one I will use so that we can accept the default setting and click on **Next**. As the disk is currently offline, I get a warning saying that the disk will be brought online and initialized as part of this process. Click on **OK** to continue.

8. You can then specify the size of the volume. If possible, split the disk into different volumes. In our case, as it's going to be used for database data files, I'm simply going to leave the disk to be the maximum size of the volume. So it will be 9.97 GB in size, which is the maximum available size. Then, click on **Next**:

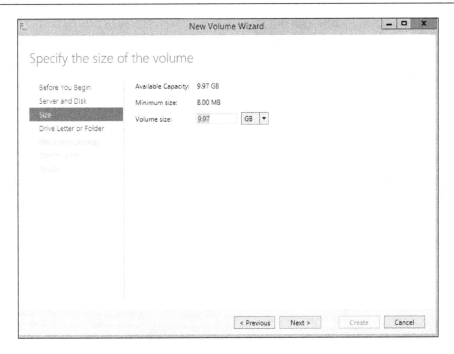

9. On the next screen, we decide whether we want the drive to be presented with its own drive letter, or if its going to form a mount point of an existing drive and take the form of a folder. I will change the letter to M and click on **Next**:

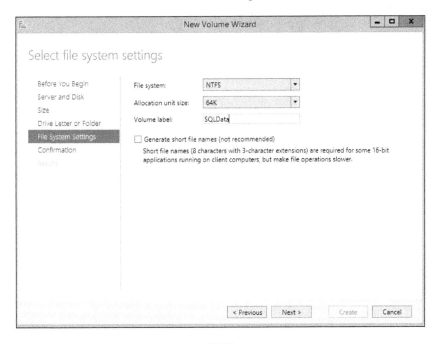

10. Then, we need to choose the **File system**, which I'm going to leave as **NTFS**. As an alternative, you could pick **ReFS**, which stands for Resilient File System. For more information on this new type of file system in Windows 2012, visit `http://msdn.microsoft.com/en-us/library/windows/desktop/hh848060(v=vs.85).aspx`. As I'm going to be using the drive for SQL Server database files, I am going to change the **Allocation unit size** to **64K**.

11. Click on **Next**, and then click on **Create** to add the drive as the disk in your Azure virtual machine. When complete, the disk will show in the filesystem:

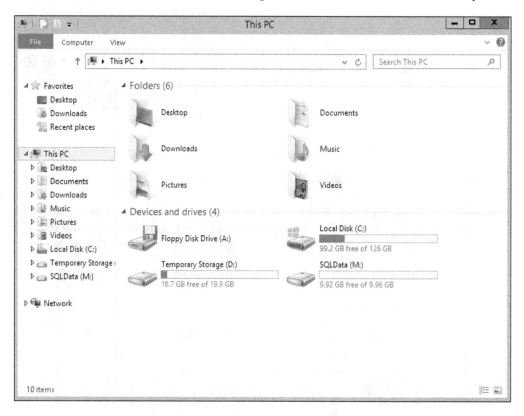

Deploying an existing server to Microsoft Azure

We have seen the process of creating a new server from scratch. What would we do with the existing physical servers or virtual servers running on an on-premises hypervisor such as ESX or Hyper-V so that we can move to the cloud? Well, the answer is relatively straightforward.

Let's assume that for the purposes of this exercise, you want to convert an existing server as it is, but with configuration changes.

In order to migrate an existing server to a Microsoft Azure virtual machine, we need to have our server's disks as VHDs. Unsurprisingly, VHDs are the disk formats that Hyper-V uses too. So, if you have a physical server, you can use your Virtual Machine Manager (VMM) that is part of System Center to perform a physical-to-virtual (P2V) migration of the server and its disks. This would need to be done on premises. There are other third-party P2V tools that could also be used to perform the migration. Alternatively, if you are using a different non-Hyper-V hypervisor, you can run a virtual-to-virtual (V2V) on the virtual machine to get the disks to the correct format.

In the Azure portal, you will create a Blob storage area to place your VHD. In the portal, click on the **Storage** option on the left-hand side menu, and choose the **New** option. Click on **Quick Create** and give your storage account a name. I have named mine gethynellisstorage:

You will then create a new container in this account. Click on the account that we just created, and click on the **Containers** option that can be found at the top of the screen. Then, click on **Create a Container**. I have named my container vhdimsages, and click on the tick icon to create the container. When it has been successfully created, you will have a storage container, and you will be able to see the storage container URL:

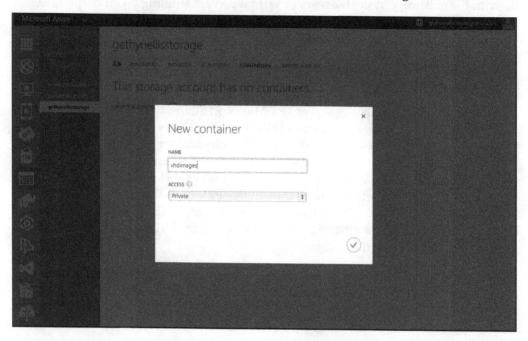

Then, you are ready to upload your .vhd file; you can place the .vhd file anywhere within the Blob storage we just created. In the following PowerShell examples, BlobStorageURL is the URL for the storage account that we created earlier. vhdimages is the container within the Blob storage we created earlier. **VHDName** is the label that appears in the management portal to identify the virtual hard disk. **PathToVHDFile** is the full path and name of the .vhd file.

From the Microsoft Azure PowerShell window, you can execute the following command:

```
Add-AzureVhd -Destination "<BlobStorageURL>/<vhdimage>/<VHDName>.vhd"
-LocalFilePath <PathToVHDFile>
```

Once uploaded, then we can add the image to our custom image list. You can perform the following steps to add an image:

1. Connect to the Azure portal, and click on the **Virtual Machines** option on the left-hand side.

2. Click on the **Images** option, and then select **Create An Image**:

3. Specify the name of the image.

4. Give it a description.

5. Specify the URL of the VHD, and you can look for this image.

6. Choose the Windows for the family operating system.

7. Click on **Open**.

8. The image will now appear in the **Images** tab of our virtual machines.

9. Then, you can create a new virtual machine, as we have done earlier in this chapter. You can select the **My Images** option and choose an image option and pick the image we just created

Summary

In this chapter, we looked at how we can create a new Windows-based virtual machine in Microsoft Azure. We looked at how we can connect to and work on the virtual machine and how we can control the virtual machine using PowerShell. Finally, we completed the chapter by converting an existing server and making it an Azure-based virtual machine.

In the next chapter, we will take a look at how we can create a Linux-based virtual machine on Microsoft's Azure cloud.

3
Deploying Linux Virtual Machines on Azure

In the previous chapter, we learned how to deploy Windows-based virtual machines to Microsoft Azure. In this chapter, we will take a look at how we can deploy non-Microsoft operating systems to Microsoft Azure. In truth, the process of Linux virtual machine deployment is similar to that of a Windows-based virtual machine, with a few minor differences. In this chapter, you will learn the following topics:

- Deploy a Linux-based virtual machine
- Connect to the new Linux virtual machine
- Learn some Linux commands to allow you to work with Linux

What is Linux?

Linux is a Unix-like operating system that has been developed by the open source movement to provide free and open source software. The key component is the Linux kernel. This was first released in the very early 1990s. I was still at school when this first form of Linux was released. It's creator was Linus Torvalds. Today, there are many flavors of Linux, and we can take a look at some of the different flavors available in Azure later in this chapter.

In the Microsoft Azure gallery of virtual machines, you can choose your Linux server from a number of options:

- Ubuntu
- CoreOS
- CentOS-based
- SUSE
- Oracle

Ubuntu

Ubuntu is a Linux-based operating system with Unity as its default desktop environment. It is based on free software and named after the Southern African philosophy of Ubuntu , which is often translated as "humanity toward others" or "the belief in a universal bond of sharing that connects all humanity."

> *"Development of Ubuntu is led by UK-based Canonical Ltd., a company owned by South African entrepreneur Mark Shuttleworth. Canonical generates revenue through the sale of technical support and other services related to Ubuntu. The Ubuntu project is publicly committed to the principles of open source development; people are encouraged to use free software, study how it works, improve upon it, and distribute it."*

CoreOS

CoreOS is a flavor of Linux that has been rearchitected for large-scale deployments. Here is a quote from the CoreOS website:

> *"CoreOS is a new Linux distribution that has been rearchitected to provide features needed to run modern infrastructure stacks. The strategies and architectures that influence CoreOS allow companies like Google, Facebook and Twitter to run their services at scale with high resilience."*

CentOS-based

CentOS is a Linux derivative based on Red Hat Linux.

Here is a quote from its website (`http://www.centos.org/about/`):

> *"The CentOS Linux distribution is a stable, predictable, manageable and reproducible platform derived from the sources of Red Hat Enterprise Linux (RHEL). We are now looking to expand on that by creating the resources needed by other communities to come together and be able to build on the CentOS Linux platform. And today we start the process by delivering a clear governance model, increased transparency and access. In the coming weeks we aim to publish our own roadmap that includes variants of the core CentOS Linux."*

SUSE

SUSE Linux is another flavor of the Linux OS, and here is a quote from its website (`https://www.suse.com/company/`):

> *"Established in 1992, SUSE, now part of Micro Focus, is the original provider of the enterprise Linux distribution and the most interoperable platform for mission-critical computing. With a portfolio centered around SUSE Linux Enterprise, we power thousands of organizations around the world across physical, virtual and cloud environments."*

Oracle

Oracle has its own flavor of Linux. Here is a quote from the Oracle website:

> *"Oracle Linux provides the latest innovations, tools, and features that enable you to innovate, collaborate, and create solutions across traditional, cloud-based, and virtual environments. Providing advanced scalability and reliability for enterprise applications and systems, Oracle Linux delivers extreme performance and is used in all x86-based Oracle Engineered Systems. Oracle Linux is free to use, free to distribute, free to update, and easy to download. It is the only Linux distribution with production support for zero-downtime kernel updates with Oracle Ksplice, allowing customers the ability to apply patches for security and other updates without a reboot, as well as providing diagnostic features for debugging kernel issues on production systems."*

Creating a Linux-based virtual machine

In order to create a Linux machine in Microsoft Azure, you will need to log in to the Microsoft Azure portal using the credentials that you would have created in *Chapter 1, Introduction to Microsoft Azure Cloud Services*.

When you have logged into the portal, click on the **Virtual Machines** link on the left-hand side of the menu, as shown in the following screenshot:

You will see the virtual machines that we created earlier in the Windows-based virtual machines. To create a Linux virtual machine, click on the **New** button at the bottom of the screen:

This will start the **Create new virtual machine wizard**, then click on the **From Gallery** option:

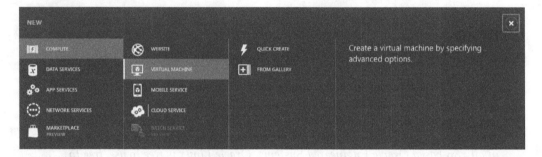

In the Azure gallery, you have several options when it comes to choosing the Linux variety or flavor that you want to install. We reviewed the options earlier in the chapter. In this example, we are going to use a CentOS-based version of Linux, which is basically a Red Hat Enterprise. I have chosen this version, as this is the one I'm familiar with, you can chose whichever version best suits your needs:

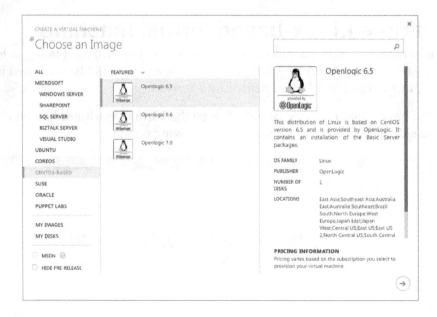

Click on the **Centos-Based** option on the left-hand side menu, then select **Openlogic 6.5** and click on the right arrow. You will be provided with the following screenshot:

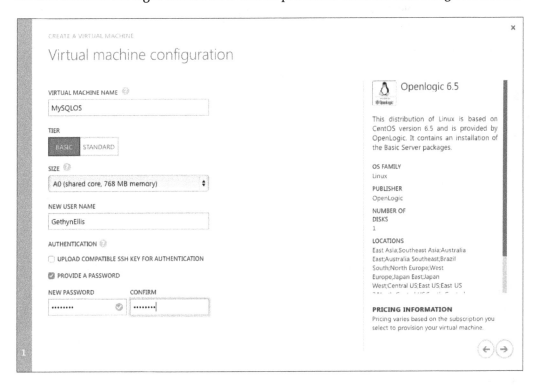

The following are the steps to configure the virtual machine:

1. Give the virtual machine a name. I have chosen the name MySQLOS, as I would likely want to use MySQL on this server.

2. Choose your **Tier** package. I have chosen **Basic**. We discussed the tier option in *Chapter 2, Creating and Deploying a Windows Virtual Machine*.

3. You can then choose the size of the virtual machine. As I have chosen the **Basic** package, I am limited to the A-size machines. Virtual machines are charged by the minute, and the size of the virtual machine you choose will dictate how much you get charged. So, choose the size that meets your requirements. "Going big early" can result in unnecessary costs.

4. You then have to provide a username. In this example, the name I chose is nice and simple to remember, GethynEllis.

5. You then need to choose an authentication method. You can choose to upload an SSH key for authentication, or you can provide a password. I chose to select the option to provide a password. You then need to enter and confirm your password, and click on the right arrow:

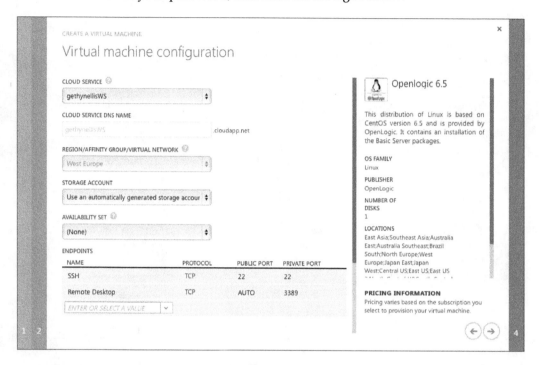

6. You can choose a cloud service, which is the container to place the virtual machine. I selected GethynEllisWS. You will have created one in the previous chapter.

7. Accept all the defaults on the screen with the exception of the endpoints to be enabled. SSH is already enabled. Click on the drop-down list, and add **Remote Desktop** to the list. You will want to pick a region that is close to your home. Click on the right arrow:

8. Accept the default settings on the final screen, including the option to **Install the VM Agent**, and then click on the tick icon to complete the wizard, and start the process of creating the virtual machine:

Azure will then start to provision the virtual machine. This process can be time consuming—you will need some patience here till the machine is created.

Working with your Linux virtual machine

With the Linux virtual machine running, you might wonder how to connect to your new Linux virtual machine, especially if you are from a Windows background. For those of you familiar with Windows, the answer is not quite the same as the Windows virtual machine we created in the earlier chapter.

Connect using Secure Shell (SSH)

Most Linux users will be used to working with the command line interface (CLI). If working with Linux is new to you, then this section will provide you with some specific information about working with Linux. You will need a SSH client to log in to your virtual machine. This needs to be installed on the computer that you wish to connect to the Linux virtual machine from.

In my case, this is going to be my Windows 7 laptop.

There are several free open source SSH clients that you can download for free. There is a comparative list on Wikipedia. You can view this comparison at:

`http://en.wikipedia.org/wiki/Comparison_of_SSH_clients.`

Two of the most popular are PuTTY and OpenSSH.

You can download PuTTY from `http://www.chiark.greenend.org.uk/~sgtatham/putty/download.html` and OpenSSH from `http://www.openssh.com`. OpenSSH is used for computers running a Linux operating system.

The following are the steps to install PuTTY:

1. I have downloaded PuTTY and copied the executable to my Windows desktop. To start, double-click on the PuTTY executable file:

2. Double-click on the PuTTY client to start it. Click on **Run** if prompted to run the software from a security warning screen:

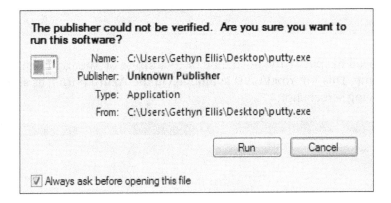

3. You will then be faced with the main PuTTY screen. There are a number of pages and options in this SSH utility. We will cover some of the basics that are needed to connect to our Linux Azure based virtual machine:

4. You need to specify the hostname or IP address of the Linux virtual machine. This information is available via the Azure portal, as shown in the following screenshot:

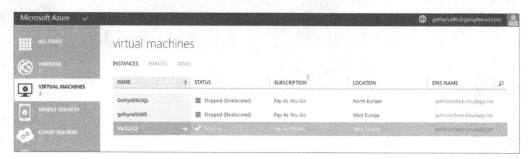

5. On the **Virtual Machines** tab, in the portal, click on the name of your Linux virtual machine. My machine is called `MySQLOS`.

6. When you click on the Linux virtual machine, click on the dashboard link at the top of the screen. Scroll down until you come across the SSH details on the left-hand side of the screen:

> SSH DETAILS
>
> gethynellisws.cloudapp.net : 22

7. So, we enter the SSH details in our PuTTY session.

8. I have entered `GethynellisWS.cloudapp.net` as the hostname and the port number as `22`.

9. Click on **Open** to start your session.

10. You need to log in using the username and password that we created earlier in the chapter, and you will be able to connect to your Linux virtual machine:

```
login as: GethynEllis
GethynEllis@gethynellisws.cloudapp.net's password:
Last login: Fri May  1 10:23:32 2015 from host86-156-135-184.range86-156.btcentr
alplus.com
[GethynEllis@MySQLOS ~]$ []
```

Connect using Remote Desktop Protocol

Now, we are able to connect using SSH. We can set up our virtual machine so that we can connect using a remote desktop session. We need to use SSH to configure this.

In this example, I have connected to the PuTTY command line interface using the login name, GethynEllis, that I created earlier. To enable the remote desktop, we need to configure the virtual machine desktop and RDP configuration. It is worth noting that working via RDP can work out to be more expensive than using the CLI, as more bandwidth is used for both uploading and downloading the Azure-based virtual machine.

To enable RDP, you will need to execute the commands in the following steps:

1. Running the following code will give you the root privileges:

   ```
   sudo -s
   ```

2. We need to install the desktop repository systems by running the following command:

   ```
   rpm -Uvh http://li.nux.ro/download/nux/dextop/el7/x86_64/nux-
   dextop-release-0-1.el7.nux.noarch.rpm
   ```

3. Next, we will install the GNOME desktop by running the following command:

   ```
   yum groupinstall "GNOME Desktop" "Graphical Administration
   Tools"
   ```

   This process can take some time, depending on your Internet connection speed. You will be prompted to continue several times during the installation; simply press *Y* to continue.

4. In this step, we will configure the virtual machine to use a graphical user interface, as opposed to the command line:

```
ln -sf /lib/systemd/system/runlevel5.target
/etc/systemd/system/default.target
```

5. Next, we will install `xrdp` by running the following command:

```
yum -y install xrdp tigervnc-server
```

6. Start the `xrdp` service by running the following command:

```
systemctl start xrdp.service
```

7. Then, enable the service using the following command:

```
systemctl enable xrdp.service
```

8. That's it, when you have enabled it, you can connect using RDP. We created the endpoint earlier. So, we can click on **Connect** tab in the portal and connect using RDP:

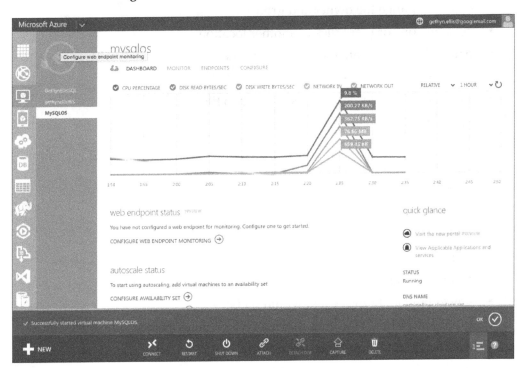

Useful Linux commands

The following is a list of commands that can help you manage your Linux infrastructure:

- **Alias**: Create an alias
- **apropos**: Search Help manual pages (man -k)
- **bash**: Bourne Again Shell
- **bzip2**: Compress or decompress named file(s)
- **cal**: Display a calendar
- **cat**: Concatenate and print (display) the content of files
- **cd**: Change directory
- **chgrp**: Change group ownership
- **chmod**: Change access permissions
- **chown**: Change file owner and group
- **cp**: Copy one or more files to another location
- **date**: Display or change the date and time
- **df**: Display free disk space
- **diff**: Display the differences between two files
- **echo**: Display a message on screen
- **env**: Display environment variables
- **exec**: Execute a command
- **exit**: Exit the shell
- **export**: Set an environment variable
- **fg**: Send a job to foreground
- **file**: Determine the file type
- **fsck**: Check and repair the file system consistency
- **gawk**: Find and replace text within file(s)
- **grep**: Search file(s) for lines that match a given pattern
- **groupadd**: Add a user security group
- **groups**: Print the group names a user is in
- **gzip**: Compress or decompress named file(s)

- **head**: Output the first part of file(s) help and display help for a built-in command
- **history**: Command to show history
- **hostname**: Print or set system name
- **id**: Print user and group IDs
- **ifconfig**: Configure a network interface
- **jobs**: List active jobs
- **kill**: Stop a process from running
- **less**: Display output one screen at a time
- **ln**: Create a symbolic link to a file
- **ls**: List information about file(s)
- **man**: Help manual
- **mkdir**: Create new folder(s)
- **more**: Display output one screen at a time
- **mv**: Move or rename files or directories
- **ping**: Test a network connection
- **ps**: Process status
- **pwd**: Print a working directory
- **rcp**: Copy files between two machines
- **rename**: Rename files
- **return**: Exit a shell function
- **rm**: Remove files
- **rmdir**: Remove folder(s)
- **rsync**: Remote file copy (Synchronize file trees)
- **scp**: Secure copy (remote file copy)
- **shutdown**: Shut down or restart linux
- **sleep**: Delay for a specified time
- **source**: Run commands from a file '.'
- **ssh**: Secure Shell client (remote login program)
- **su**: Substitute user identity
- **sudo**: Execute a command as another user
- **symlink**: Make a new name for a file

- **tail**: Output the last part of file
- **tar**: Tape archiver
- **touch**: Change file timestamps
- **useradd**: Create a new user account
- **users**: List the users currently logged in
- **wc**: Print byte, word, and line counts
- **whereis**: Search the user's $path, manual pages and source files for a program
- **which**: Search the user's $path for a program file
- **who**: Print all usernames currently logged in
- **whoami**: Print the current user ID and name ('id -un')
- **wget**: Send web pages or files via HTTP, HTTPS or FTP
- **write**: Send a message to another user
- **.**: A command script in the current shell
- **!!**: Run the last command again
- **###**: Comment / Remark

Summary

In this chapter, we looked at how we can create and configure a Linux-based virtual machine in Microsoft Azure's cloud. We looked at the different flavors of Linux available and how to create the virtual machine. We also looked at how we can use the command line interface and PuTTY, how we can configure and connect via RDP to work with Linux, and we provided you with a list of useful commands. In the next chapter, we will take a look at how you can manage and monitor your virtual machine.

4

Virtual Networks

In this chapter, we will take a look at how we can configure, set up, and deploy a virtual network that will allow our Azure-based virtual machines to interact and communicate with each other in the cloud and potentially communicate with our on-premises servers too. In this chapter, you will learn the following topics:

- The definition of an Azure Virtual Network
- The benefits of a virtual network
- How to configure a virtual network
- Cross-premises virtual networking
- How to move an existing virtual machine to a virtual network

What is an Azure Virtual Network?

An **Azure Virtual Network (VNET)** is something that you will create in Microsoft Azure. The VNET will allow virtual machines and the other resources that are part of the VNET to communicate with each other privately. It is the VNET that provides this communication function. Without a VNET, or if a virtual machine resides outside the VNET, communication with other resources would not be possible. The VNET offers another level of abstraction, and thus, another layer of extra security.

VNET and virtual networking are useful and important if you want to make use of both your on-premises network, infrastructure, and resources in Microsoft's Azure cloud.

When deciding whether you need a virtual network or not, you will have to consider what your end goal is and what exactly you want to achieve. It's important to get the network set up correctly the first time, as it is much easier to deploy new virtual machines to a network than it is to add existing virtual machines to the network later.

There is no out-of-the-box design that will work and fit all environments. Having said that, there are three basic categories of network configuration for you to consider:

- No VNET
- Cloud-only VNET
- Cross-premises VNET

The first two categories on the list are pretty self-descriptive. No VNET means that you don't have a VNET, and your cloud-based resources sit as standalone entities. A cloud-only VNET is a network based in Azure that allows your cloud-based resources to communicate with each other. If you have an entirely cloud-based solution and you want the resources to be able to communicate with each other, then a cloud-only VNET might be something for you to consider.

The cross-premises option will allow you to build a hybrid network, extending your on-premises network in the Microsoft cloud.

Azure virtual machines and services acquire their network settings during the deployment; therefore, it is best to know whether you need a virtual network before the deployment, as you can't just move your VM to the VNET. You can, however, redeploy your virtual machine and cloud services, but this will result in downtime while the redeployment occurs. You might have noticed that the virtual machines we have created so far have not been deployed to a virtual network; we will take a look at the process of redeployment in this chapter.

The benefits of virtual networks

If you decide that creating a virtual network is the right thing for your environment, then there are a number of additional benefits for you to take advantage of. By creating a virtual network, you will be able to perform the following functions:

- **Name resolution**: Implementing and configuring DNS will allow you to work with your virtual machines and other resources by referring to their hostname, which is much more user-friendly than the IP address port combination you would need without the DNS.

- **Increased security**: You will benefit from the increased security and isolation. Resources that are part of a virtual network will be able to communicate and access each other. Any virtual machine that resides outside the virtual network will not have this ability. So, your virtual network resources have an extra isolation layer.

- **Include more resources in a trust and security boundary**: Instead of your security boundary being a single virtual machine, you can expand this boundary to all the virtual machines in the network. If you create several virtual machines in the virtual network, they will be able to communicate with each other securely.

- **Extend on-premises network to the cloud**: You can join virtual machines that reside in the Azure cloud to your on-premises domain. This allows you to expand your on-premises infrastructure to the Microsoft Azure cloud platform.

- **Static private IP addresses**: Virtual machines that reside in your virtual network can have static IP addresses.

The virtual network topology

There are two main types of virtual network configurations; one that will remain completely in the Azure cloud known as cloud-only, and the other one known as a cross-premises network that will allow both cloud-based and on-premises resources to communicate. We will discuss both the types here.

A cloud-only virtual network

Cloud-only virtual networks are useful when you have an entire system and its various tiers that reside in Azure, and there is no need for these virtual machines to communicate with other resources in different networks. Cloud-only virtual networks are virtual networks that reside entirely in Microsoft Azure. There is no need for a VNET gateway to be able connect back to your on-premises network or to another virtual network in Microsoft Azure.

There are some subtle differences when it comes to setting up and configuring a cloud-only virtual network compared to a cross-premises network configuration. With a cloud-only virtual network, you will be able to connect to virtual machines and other resources from the endpoints rather than using a VPN connection:

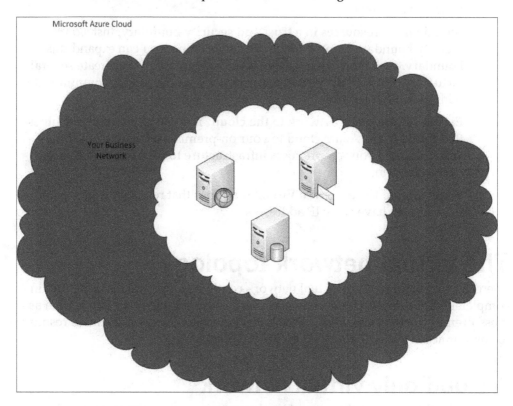

It is a simple process to create a cloud-only virtual network. It's relatively straightforward, as you don't need to worry about coordinating your IP address ranges with the ranges on your local on-premises network or with the IP addresses in other cloud-based networks. As there is no connectivity between other on-premises networks, there is no requirement to set up and configure a VPN device.

Switching between a cloud-only network and a cross-premises configuration is not a simple process. It is more complicated than adding a gateway to your VNET. The reason for the complication is that the IP address ranges that you select cannot overlap with the ranges that are on your local network. If this situation does arise, you will need to create a new virtual network with the required settings and redeploy the virtual machines to the new virtual network. We will discuss how to do this later in the chapter.

A cross-premises virtual network

The ability to create a network that spans from your on-premises network and into the cloud is referred to as a cross-premises virtual network. Cross-premises connectivity provides you and your organization with several benefits and a great deal of flexibility when it comes to your infrastructure.

You will be able to create multisite configurations, VNET-to-VNET configurations, or a combination of configuration types. The major benefit is, clearly, the ability to expand your local on-premises network to the cloud, providing you with an infrastructure solution that provides the flexibility and dynamic responsiveness that cloud offers.

A Virtual Private Network (VPN) is a device that is needed to create a cross-premises network. This device is then used to establish a secure connection with the Azure Virtual Network.

Cross-premises network configurations are sometimes called hybrid solutions. These are generally more complicated to implement and require more planning and preparation than cloud-only configurations. In a large organization, it is likely that elements of the cross-premises configuration will need involvement from the other teams and other people, including your network team because some of the activities will involve coordinating with the network routing, as well as configuring VPN devices.

There are three types of cross-premises network that you can set up in Microsoft Azure:

- Site-to-site
- Point-to-site
- ExpressRoute

A **site-to-site** virtual network allows you to create a secure connection between your Azure-based virtual network and your on-premises local network.

To do this, you will need:

- At least one publicly visible IP address
- A VPN device — Windows Server 2012 Routing and Remote Access service
- Extra machines for testing
- A subscription to Azure

This VPN device is configured to create a secure connection with the Azure Virtual Network Gateway. When the connection is established, the virtual machines and servers on your local on-premises network and the resources that are located in your Azure cloud-based virtual network can communicate directly:

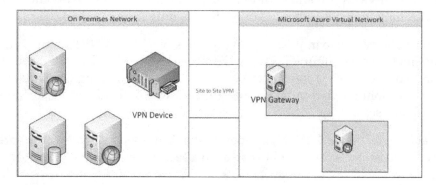

With a site-to-site configuration, there is no requirement for each local computer on your premises to establish a connection with the cloud-based resources. They will instead make use of the dedicated VPN device.

Site-to-site configurations are generally used when you make use of a scaled-up cloud-based environment and have several on-premises resources that need to access resources in the cloud. This will remove the need for you to configure each and every local device.

A **point-to-site** configuration will also create a secure VPN connection to the Azure Virtual Network. The difference between a point-to-site and site-to-site configuration is that the point-to-site setup does not use a specific device, instead each client will have a VPN client installed and will establish a connection individually:

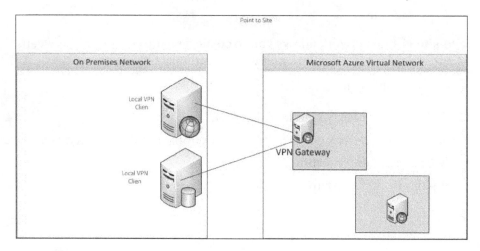

A point-to-site configuration can be useful when:

- You have a small number of clients.
- You work remotely and you want to connect to the cloud VNET from a remote location.
- You don't have a suitable VPN device that meets the necessary requirements. You can find the information on the device requirements at https://msdn. microsoft.com/en-us/library/azure/jj156075.aspx

Microsoft Azure also has something called **ExpressRoute**. This is similar to site-to-site connectivity. It lets you create private connections between the Azure data centers and infrastructures that are on your premises. ExpressRoute connections don't communicate with the public Internet, and as such, offer a number of benefits compared to a site-to-site connection that goes over the Internet:

- They are more reliable
- They have potentially faster speeds
- They have lower latencies
- They have higher security

Configuring a virtual network

In this section, we will take a look at the tasks that need to be completed to create and configure a virtual network.

Creating a cloud-only virtual network

We know the benefits of creating a virtual network. Azure-based virtual machines and other resources within the network can communicate securely with each other. Creating a dedicated cloud-only virtual network is a very simple and straightforward process, as there are no additional complications, such as configuring a VPN device.

Now, your cloud-only virtual network has been created. Once you have created your cloud-only virtual network, you can add new VMs and PaaS instances to it. It is worth noting here that the process of adding an existing virtual machine resource to a VNET is not a simple process, as you will see this in a later section, so ensure that you plan your virtual networks correctly to begin with. When you create a new virtual machine, you will be able to specify the virtual network it belongs to.

You will need the following information to create your cloud-only virtual network:

- **Name**: You can create whatever name you'd like to, but I would recommend that you use sensible naming conventions; maybe something that allows you to quickly identify what the VNET is used for, particularly, if your environment is a large one. You'll need this virtual network name when you deploy your virtual machines, so it's best not to have a name that is too complicated.

- **Location:** The region you choose is directly related to the Microsoft data center, where your virtual machines are made to reside when you deploy them to this virtual network. Let's say most of your businesses and customers are located in Northern Europe. You might make a decision to locate your cloud-based infrastructure in the Northern European data center (which, at the time of writing, is based in Dublin). Select this region. It's important to note that you can't change the region associated with your virtual network after you create it.

- **DNS information**: This is optional and would only be used if you have to set up the DNS.

The following steps will create a cloud-only virtual network:

1. Log in to the Azure portal using the credentials we created in *Chapter 1, Introduction to Microsoft Azure Cloud Services*.

2. Scroll to the bottom of the left-hand side menu until you find the **Networks** option, and then click on it. You will see a screen similar to the following screenshot:

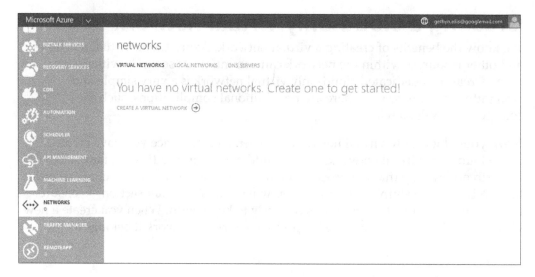

3. Click on the **Create a Virtual Network** link listed on the virtual network tab in the detail pane. The network configuration wizard will start.

4. On the **Virtual Network Details** page, enter the following information:

    ° **Name**: Enter the name of the virtual network. I have named my network GRESol:

    ° **Location**: Select the region for your network from the drop-down list

5. The DNS screen is the next screen that appears. We will enter the DNS and VPN connectivity information on this screen; in this case, we can accept all the defaults, as we don't need to make any changes for a cloud-only configuration. Click on the right arrow to move on to the next page. In the cloud, Azure provides the basic name resolution for your virtual network:

6. On the **Virtual Network Address Spaces** screen, you don't need to make any changes, so we will accept the defaults. You would only make changes here if you required a certain internal IP address range for your virtual machine, or if you wanted to create a specific subnet for the virtual machines that will receive a static IP address:

The preceding screenhot shows where you have to specify the range of the IP addresses that your virtual machines will be allocated with when they get deployed to the virtual network. These IP addresses are for internal communication on the virtual network.

In this situation, we aren't going to connect this private virtual network to your on-premises network. If you want to create a connection for your on-premises network, using a cross-premises VPN configuration, you need to plan and coordinate the IP address ranges to be used to avoid any issues later.

7. Click on the tick icon on the lower right-hand side of the wizard to complete the wizard, and Azure will begin to create your network. When the new virtual network has been created successfully, you will see it listed on the network page of the Azure Management Portal, as being created.

8. With your virtual network now created, you can create a virtual machine infrastructure that uses the virtual networks. Be sure to select the **From Gallery** option when creating a new virtual machine in order to have the option to select your virtual network.

Redeploying virtual machines into a virtual network

The virtual machines that we have deployed so far are not part of our virtual network. How do we go about moving a virtual machine to a different network? There is no easy way to move an existing virtual machine to the network. The process involves using the VHD of the virtual machine that you want to include in the virtual network, and then creating a new virtual machine based on the VHDs of the old virtual machine.

In this section, I am going to move the GethynEllisSQL virtual machine that we created in an earlier chapter to the GRESol network:

1. Log in to the Azure portal.

2. Click on the **Virtual Machines** tab in the portal:

3. Click on the virtual machine you want to redeploy into the new virtual network. In this case, click on the GethynEllisSQL virtual machine.

4. Click on the **Dashboard** link at the top of the page:

5. When the dashboard opens, scroll to the bottom of the page, where you will see the disk information of this virtual machine. There is an option for you to copy the path of the disk. Make a note of this path for future purposes. Use the file that has a built-in copy function so that you can copy the values to your clipboard. Mine are `https://portalvhds3s12v9t69rdb9.blob.core.windows.net/vhds/GethynEllisSQL-GethynEllisSQL-2014-11-24.vhd` and `https://portalvhds3s12v9t69rdb9.blob.core.windows.net/vhds/SQLServerData.vhd`:

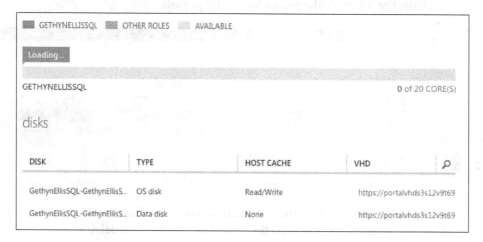

6. This step needs to be completed with some caution because we will be deleting the virtual machine. The deletion is the important bit. You will delete the virtual machine without deleting the disks. While you are still in the dashboard, click on the **Delete** button at the bottom of the screen.

   Once you have clicked on the **Delete** button, you need to select the **Keep the attached disks** option.

7. You will be prompted to click on **Yes**, and the virtual machine will be deleted.

8. You need to confirm that the virtual machine has been deleted. You can do this by clicking on the disk page at the top of the screen. You will see the disk(s) that were attached to the virtual machine are now not showing as attached to a virtual machine:

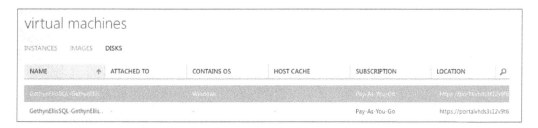

9. Next, you need to create a new virtual machine with the same name using the Windows gallery.

10. Then, choose **New** from the action bar at the bottom of the screen.

11. Select the **From Gallery** option:

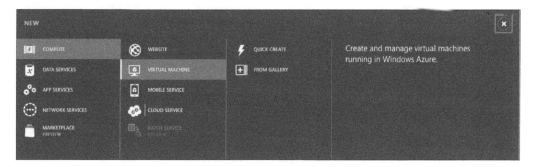

12. On the gallery screen, choose the **My Disks** option in the list, and you will see the disk, which we deleted, that was previously attached to the virtual machine. In this case, it is the only disk listed here, as I had not created any other data disks for the virtual machine:

13. Click on the right arrow.

14. Give the virtual machine a name. I will keep the same name
    GethynEllisSQL. This is to avoid any confusion and reconfiguration of
    the virtual machine after the name has been changed.

15. Choose an appropriate tier package, I have selected basic **A0**, and then click
    on right arrow:

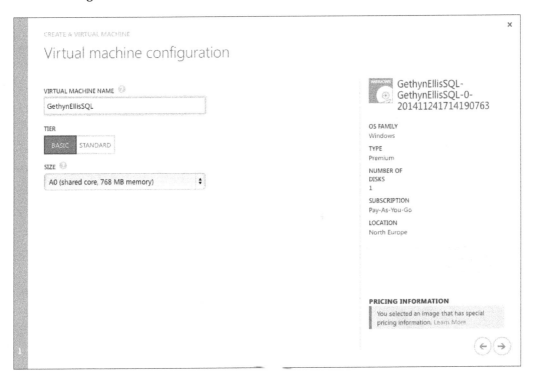

16. You will then be able to select the new virtual network from the
    Region/Affinity Group/ Virtual Network drop-down list. Click on
    next, and then **Finish**, to provision the new virtual machine:

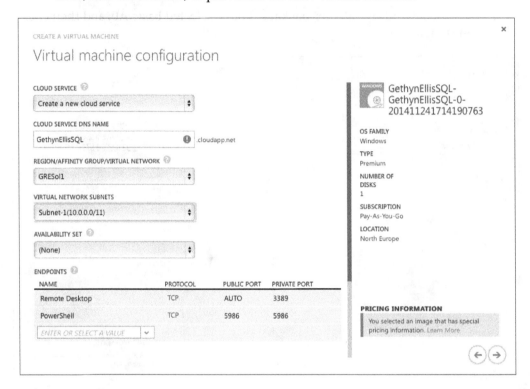

When the virtual machine is provisioned, you have moved your virtual machine to
your new network.

Configuring a cross-premises virtual network

In this section, you will gain an understanding of the steps needed to configure
a point-to-site VPN. This is the type of cross-premises network configuration
you would use when you don't have an appropriate VPN device for a site-to-site
connection, or you only have a very small number of clients that you need to connect
to. The process is similar but not identical for a site-to-site configuration. You will
probably need advice from the network administrator when it comes to configuring
this for a production environment.

This task can be broken down into three major steps:

- Configuring the virtual network with a dynamic gateway
- Creating the certificates
- Deploying the VPN client

Configuring the virtual network with a dynamic gateway

The first of these steps is to create a new network with the appropriate options selected in the Azure Management Portal:

1. Log in to the management portal and scroll to the **Networks** section on the right-hand side menu list.
2. Click on the **New** button at the bottom left-hand corner of the screen.
3. You should have **Network Services Virtual Network** chosen by default. Click on the **Custom Create** tab.
4. This will start the **Create a Virtual Network** Wizard.
5. Choose a name, I have selected the name GREWEU.
6. Choose a location, I have selected **Western Europe**. Click on the right arrow. You should choose a location where you want your virtual machine to reside. I live in Western Europe, so this is the option I have selected.
7. Here, you can specify your enterprise/company DNS servers if you wish. You can leave the DNS fields blank if you don't want to specify a specific server here.

8. Check the box titled **Configure a point-to-site VPN**. Note that you can also configure a site-to-site connection if you wish. When you check the point-to-site box, the network diagram will change at the bottom of the screen. Click on the right arrow to continue:

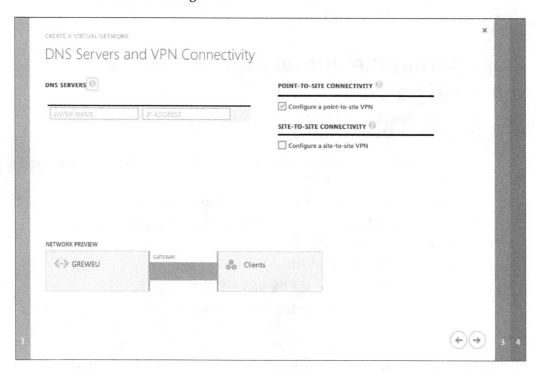

9. On the next page, we will specify the IP address range that will be reserved for our cross-premises clients. These are the IP addresses that they will be allocated when they connect via VPN. I have accepted the defaults here, which will give me plenty of available addresses for my needs. Click on the right arrow to continue.

10. The final screen is the **Virtual Network Address Space** screen, where you can specify the address range that you can use for your virtual machine. I am going to accept the defaults, but you may want to enter different values for the address space field.

11. You need to click on the **Add Gateway Subnet** button to add it. Click on the tick icon when complete.

12. Once the network has been created, we need to create a dynamic routing gateway. On the networks page in the management portal, click on the network we just created and navigate to the **Dashboard** tab.

13. At the bottom of the dashboard page, there is an option **Create Gateway**. Click on the link. You will be prompted to answer whether you are sure you want to create a gateway, then click on **Yes**. Just a word of warning that it can take up to 15 minutes to create the gateway.

Creating certificates

You will need to create a self-signed root certificate. Creating this certificate is outside the scope of this book. However, the link `http://datacenteroverlords.com/2012/03/01/creating-your-own-ssl-certificate-authority/` walks you through creating and signing your route certificate using OpenSSL. You can also use the Makecert executable that comes with Visual Studio.

I used the following code at Visual Studio Tools Command Prompt (which I run as an administrator) to generate a root certificate:

```
makecert -sky exchange -r -n "CN=GethynEllis" -pe -a sha1 -len 2048 -
ss My "GethynEllis.cer"
```

With your root certificate created, we will now upload the certificate to the management portal:

- You still need to be logged in to the management portal, and you should be in the network option on the left-hand side of the screen

- With your network selected, change the tab at the top of the screen to the certificates option

- Click on the link to upload a root certificate

- Click on the **Browse** button, and navigate to the location of your root certificate and click on **Upload**

The next task is to generate and install the client certificates. The link `http://datacenteroverlords.com/2012/03/01/creating-your-own-ssl-certificate-authority/` walks you through creating these certificates using OpenSSL. To do this, install the client certificate.

I used the `makecert.exe` file in this code that I ran from a Visual Studio Tools command prompt (which I run as an administrator):

```
makecert.exe -n "CN=ClientGRE" -pe -sky exchange -m 96 -ss My -in
"GethynEllis" -is my -a sha1
```

Configuring the VPN client

Finally, with all the necessary certificates created, you can configure the VPN client on the on-premises machine that is going to connect to your Azure Virtual Network.

On the dashboard page of the virtual network in the management portal, you will see some downloads. Download the one that best suits your setup.

When you have the executable downloaded, you can install it locally on the computer that you want to connect to. Having installed the client tool, navigate to it and connect to the VPN.

Summary

In this section, we looked at how we can create a virtual network in Azure. We looked at how we can approach moving an existing virtual machine to a new virtual network, and what is needed to configure a point-to-site connectivity for hybrid networks that allow you to combine your on-premises network with your cloud-based resources. In the next chapter, we will take a look at how we can monitor the performance of the cloud-based resources.

5
Managing and Monitoring Virtual Machines

So far, we have created some virtual machines in Azure, and we have looked at both Linux and Windows-based virtual machines. We have connected our machines via a virtual network. That's it, over to Microsoft now to look after them for us! Well, not quite. With infrastructure as a service, you will still need to monitor your servers to ensure both availability and performance. This is especially true if you build a hybrid environment that spans your on-premises infrastructure in the cloud. In this chapter, we will take a look at how we can set up monitoring in our Azure-based virtual machines.

In this chapter, you will learn the following topics:

- Monitoring Cloud Services using the Azure portal
- Configuring monitoring for Cloud Services
- Alerting for Cloud Services
- Adding metrics to the metrics table
- Other monitoring tools

Monitoring cloud services using the Azure portal

So far in this book, we have looked at how we can create Cloud Services, such as virtual machines and virtual networks, to allow us to run our infrastructure in the cloud. In this section, we will discuss how to go about monitoring your infrastructure.

By default, Azure provides minimal monitoring for any new cloud-based services that you create. This data is provided by the host operating system for virtual the machines that are running on the system. As these are minimal metrics, they are limited to the following:

- The CPU percentage
- Network in
- Network out
- Disk read throughput (Disk Read Bytes/sec)
- Disk write throughput (Disk Write Bytes/sec)

It might be that these are enough for you, and you can get by with your day-to-day needs with just these. However, it is likely that you will need additional information about your services, especially if you are running production servers in the cloud.

By configuring verbose monitoring, you will be provided with additional data and metrics based on your virtual machine's performance, including data from within the virtual machine itself, not just the counters provided by the host. A more detailed metrics will enable you to more closely analyze issues that occur during your production operations.

The following information about monitoring information is correct at the time of writing and available on the Microsoft website:

> *"By default, performance counter data from role instances is sampled and transferred from the role instance at 3-minute intervals. When you enable verbose monitoring, the raw performance counter data is aggregated for each role instance and across role instances for each role at intervals of 5 minutes, 1 hour, and 12 hours. The aggregated data is purged after 10 days."*

When you enable verbose monitoring, the data collection method changes a little; the aggregated monitoring data is stored in tables, which are stored in your storage account. Be aware that the extra storage for the extra data comes with an additional cost. In order to enable more detailed monitoring, you will need a storage account. You can configure a connection string for the diagnostic data that links to your storage account. You can use different storage accounts for the different roles that you deploy.

It is worth noting that more detailed monitoring or verbose monitoring will cost you more, as you need additional storage to store the data, and your storage costs will increase. Not only your data transfer, but your storage transactions will also increase. Minimal monitoring, which you get by default does not require a storage account.

Configuring monitoring for cloud services

In this section, we will take a look at the process that we need to follow in order to configure either verbose (detailed) or minimal monitoring using the Azure portal. In order to turn on verbose monitoring, Azure Diagnostic needs to be enabled, and a diagnostic connection string needs to be configured to allow Azure Diagnostics to access and write to the storage account that will hold the performance data.

Prerequisites

There are some prerequisites that are needed before we can configure monitoring for Cloud Services. They are as follows:

Creating a storage account

By creating a storage account in Azure, you will get a secure location that allows you to access and store data in the cloud. A storage account will provide you with a unique namespace to store your data, and it is only available to the account owner by default.

There are two types of Azure storage accounts:

- **Standard account**: This includes Blob, Table, File, and Queue storage
- **Premium storage account**: This is used for Azure virtual machine disks

We will need a standard account for our diagnostic data.

As I mentioned earlier, and on several occasions throughout the book, you will be billed based on the resources that you use and this is also true for storage account costs. The cost of your storage will depend on the following factors:

- **Storage capacity**: This refers to the amount of storage you are using to store data. The cost is determined by how much data you can hold and how it is replicated.
- **Data replication**: This determines how many copies of your data is maintained and where in the world these copies are located.
- **Amount of transactions**: This refers to how much you read and write to the storage account.

- **Bandwidth (data egress)**: This is about transferring data out of a particular Azure region; I think of a region as a data center. If your data is accessed by an application that is not running in the same region, then you are charged for data egress.

As you can see, the more verbose your diagnostics information, the more the frequency with which it is collected, and if you have applications connecting to it from a range of sites, this will again impact on your storage costs.

Azure storage replication options

When we configure our storage account in the next section, we will be prompted to select a **Replication** option. **Geo-redundant** is the default option and offers the most resilience, but what you choose will very much depend on the value you place in the information being stored in the account. As this will be used to store the diagnostics information, and if you are not so concerned about your data being durable and not too bothered about whether some of the data is not recoverable for whatever reason, you can keep the costs down by choosing a different replication option. The reason for replication is to ensure durability along with high availability that allows Azure to meet its service-level agreements in the event of a hardware failure.

The replication options include the following:

- **Locally redundant storage (LRS)**: This provides and maintains three copies of your data. LRS is replicated three times within a single facility in a single region. LRS protects you from normal hardware failures; however, there are some drawbacks, as it does not protect you from the failure of a single facility. So, if you lose the data center, you lose your data. LRS is offered at a discount, so this should be the cheapest option for your data. This might be perfectly acceptable to you for your diagnostic data.

- **Zone redundant storage replication (ZRS)**: This also maintains three copies of your data. ZRS is replicated three times across two to three data centers, either within a single region or across two regions; therefore, it provides higher durability than LRS. ZRS ensures that your data is durable within a single region. ZRS provides a higher level of durability than LRS, but not as much as geo-redundant replication.

- **Geo redundant storage (GRS)**: This is the default option when you create it. GRS maintains six copies of your data. Your storage account data is replicated three times within the primary region, and on top of this, it is also replicated three times in a secondary region, which will potentially be hundreds of miles away from the primary region thus, providing the highest level of durability. In the event of a failure in the primary region, Azure storage will failover to the secondary region. GRS ensures that your data is durable in two separate regions, and it provides a proper disaster recovery.

- **Read access-geo redundant storage (RA-GRS)**: This provides all of the benefits of geo redundant storage listed earlier; however, it goes a stage further and allows read access to data in the secondary region in the event that the primary region becomes unavailable. Read access-geo redundant storage is recommended for maximum availability in addition to durability.

The steps to create a storage account

The following steps will demonstrate how to create a storage account. I will use a single storage account to hold the diagnostic information:

1. Log in to the management portal. You can use the credentials that we used in *Chapter 1, Introduction to Microsoft Azure Cloud Services*.

2. From the left-hand side menu, click on **Storage**. In the following screenshot, you can see that I have a few storage accounts that have been created previously, as a result of the creation of the various virtual machines we have been working with so far:

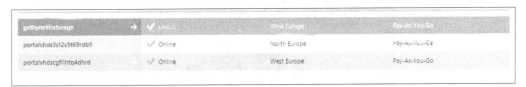

3. Click on the **New** button at the bottom of the screen.

4. This will start the **Create Storage Account** wizard, click on the **Quick Create** button:

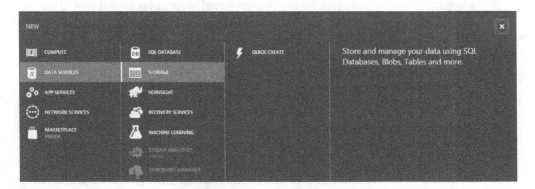

5. You will then need to enter a URL name. Note that you can only use lowercase letters and numbers for the name of the storage account. In this case, I have selected `gethynellisdiaginfo`:

6. In the **Location/Affinity Group** section, select the storage account location. Ideally, it should be close to you in terms of geography. I have chosen my affinity group, **gethynelliscom**. This is an affinity group that I created for the purpose of this book. An affinity group is useful to ensure that your cloud-based resources are located in the same region, and they are close to each other.

7. In the **Replication** drop-down list, select the desired level of replication for your storage account. An explanation of the options can be found above the recommended and default replication option, which is called **Geo-Redundant** replication. This option provides maximum durability for your data. However, in order to maintain a minimum exposure to the cost, I will chose LRS. What you chose for your data depends on the value and importance you place on this data. Some people will consider this very valuable in the management of their infrastructure, while others might not be concerned if this data is not as durable and well protected as other business data.

8. Click on the **Create Storage Account** button to create the storage account. Azure will the create your storage account:

Once we have created the storage account, we'll enable Azure Diagnostics in our virtual machine.

Enabling Azure Diagnostics in a virtual machine

The Azure portal is being upgraded all the time, and at the time of writing, a new portal is available in the preview. This portal has new advances in Azure development and includes the Azure extension model. It allows you, among other things, to configure your virtual machine for more verbose and detailed diagnostic information.

So, to do this in Azure, you need to perform the following steps:

1. Log in to the management portal, using your credentials that we created in *Chapter 1, Introduction to Microsoft Azure Cloud Services*.

2. At the time of writing, the **New Portal** is not the default option. It is available in the preview. So, we need to switch to this view. Click on your account information. Usually, your e-mail address is at the top right-hand corner of the screen. Now, click on **Switch to new portal**:

3. You will see a screen that looks similar to the following screenshot. Note that you can still see the preview markings on the screen:

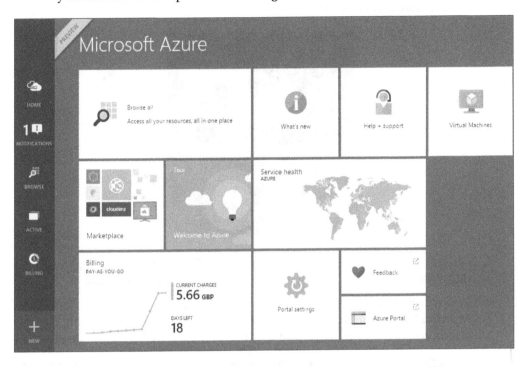

4. On the left-hand side menu, you will notice a **Browse** button. Click on the **Browse** button, and then scroll down and locate the **Virtual machines** option:

5. Click on the virtual machine you want to configure for verbose diagnostic data collection; in this case, it will be `GethynEllisSQL`.

6. You will then see some information about the virtual machine. Click on the **Monitoring** section to display the monitoring properties. Depending on your screen resolution, you may need to scroll to the right to see these details:

7. Click on the **Diagnostics** option, which can be found on the top right-hand side of the screen, next to the **Add Alert** button.

8. Change its **Status** to **On** and a lot more options will appear for you.

9. You need to select the storage account that we created earlier to ensure that the diagnostic information gets stored in the correct place.

10. As this is a SQL Server, I want to enable the SQL Server diagnostic information, so I need to check the box that is next to **SQL metrics**, and click on **Save** and **OK** to complete the configuration:

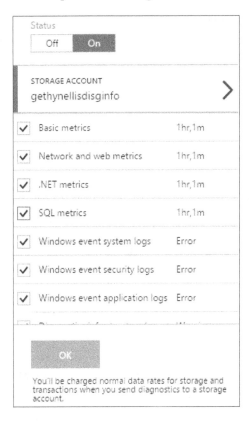

Adding metrics

You can use the Azure Management Portal for monitoring your virtual machine's performance too, without configuring the storage account and deploying an application. It doesn't record diagnostics information in as much detail as verbose monitoring; however, it can provide you with a view of your virtual machine metrics. In order to view this information, you need to perform the following steps:

1. Log in to the Azure portal using the account and credentials that we created in *Chapter 1*, *Introduction to Microsoft Azure Cloud Services*.

2. From the left-hand side menu, click on the **Virtual Machines** option. Currently, I have created three virtual machines. These are currently in a powered off state:

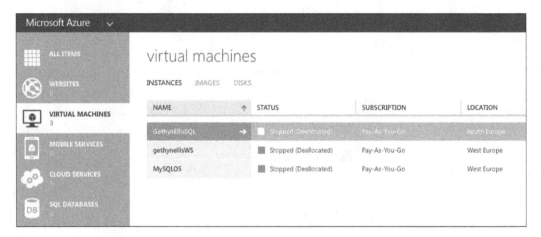

3. My virtual machine has not yet started. In order to use the resources, the virtual machine must be in a powered on state, so I need to select **Start** from the options at the bottom of the screen, and click on **Yes** when prompted to start the virtual machine. The virtual machine may take a few seconds to start up.

4. When the virtual machine has started, click on the virtual machine in the main detail pane, this will take you to the virtual machine dashboard:

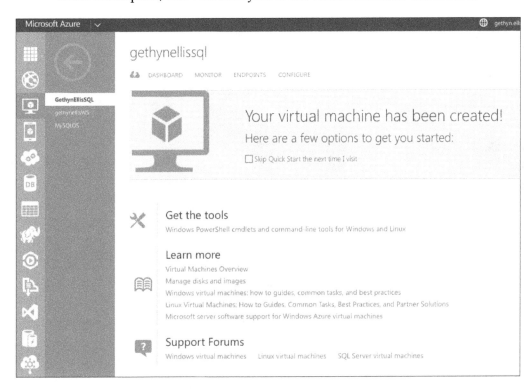

5. Click on the **Dashboard** link at the top of the screen, and this will give you an overview of the performance of your virtual machines, along with some other options about the machine and its configuration.

6. Next to the **Dashboard** option is the **Monitor** option. Click on the **Monitor** option to display the default monitor settings:

7. As you can see, we have all the metrics selected. We can go back and view the historical data by clicking on the drop-down list in the top right-hand corner. You can view 1 hour, 24 hours, or 7 days worth of data with basic monitoring. You can see from the 24 hour view that my virtual machine has been powered off for most of the day:

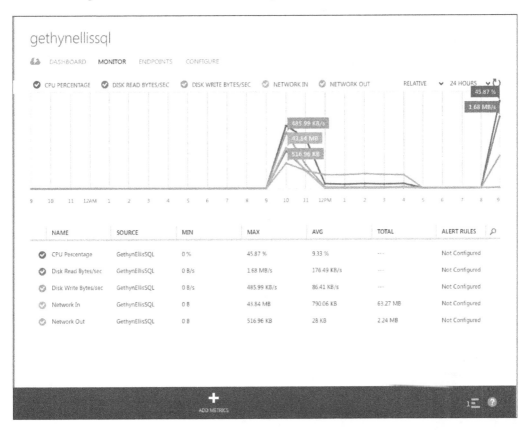

8. You can add and remove metrics by clicking on the **Add Metric** button at the bottom of the page, and select the metrics you wish to display. When you click on the check mark, the screen will refresh, displaying the new metrics that we added. You can click on the check mark in the circle beside each metric to turn the metrics on and off:

The following screenshot shows you the new display with the appropriate metrics selected:

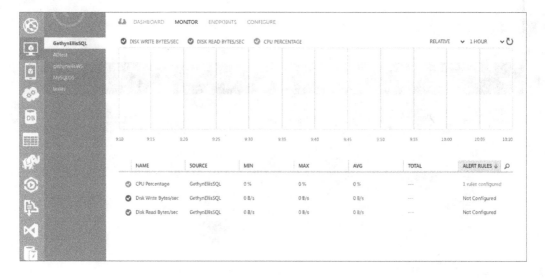

Management services

With the **Management Services** option, we can set up alerts and also take a look at the operational logs.

Alerts

With the metrics in place, you need to find a way to let us know whether something is wrong or needs the attention of an administrator.

For the metrics we have configured, we are able to set up alerts. If a certain condition is met, Azure will let you know that something is wrong with the virtual machine.

The alerts will make you aware of the issues and also allow you to do some capacity planning. Do you need to scale your cloud infrastructure to cope with the increasing demands for computing services?

Here, we will set up some alerts based on the metrics we have set up for one of our virtual machines. We will use the SQL Server virtual machine and run the code – bad code – against the virtual machine to chew up enough Azure resources to make the alert fire.

Here, assume that all the basic monitoring counters have been enabled for the virtual machine, GethynEllisSQL. The basic monitoring counters are as follows:

- **Network In**
- **Network Out**
- **The CPU percentage**
- **Disk Write Bytes/sec**
- **Disk Read Bytes/sec**

When it comes to virtual machine monitoring, you can set up rules and alerts for all of these metrics. For GethynEllisSQL, we will focus on the CPU percentage.

With nearly all the products that Microsoft produces, there is often more than one way of implementing something. This is also true with alerts in Azure. You can configure alerts in the management portal, and you can extend monitoring using tools, such as Azure Automation and System Center 2012 Operation Manager (SCOM). We will use the **Management Services** option in the portal.

The following steps will create an alert on the `GethynEllisSQL` virtual machine:

1. From the left-hand side menu, scroll down until you get to the **Management Services** option:

2. With the **Alert** option selected, which is at the top of the screen, you should see a details pane that looks similar to the following screenshot:

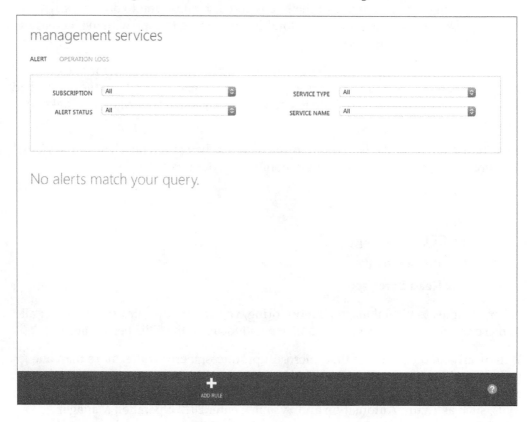

3. As you can see from the preceding screenshot, currently, there are no alerts configured. To configure an alert, click on the **Add Rule** button on the bottom menu bar.

4. Once the **Create Alert Rule** wizard starts:

    ° You need to provide a name, I have entered `CPU High`

    ° You need to provide a description, I have entered `Check for high CPU usage on SQL VM`

    ° Select **Virtual Machine** from the **Service Type** drop-down list

    ° In this case, choose the appropriate virtual machine from the **Service Name** drop-down list to create an alert on `GethynEllisSQL`:

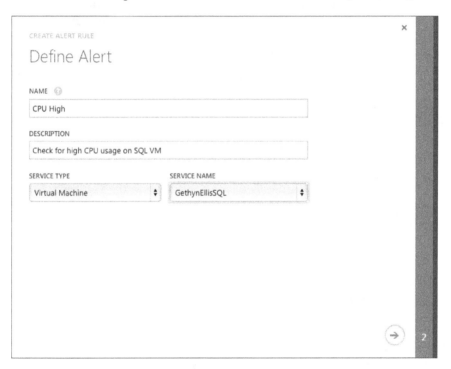

5. Click on the right arrow, and you can set up the following metrics for the alert:

    ° I have chosen **CPU Percentage** as the **Metric**

    ° Next, I have chosen **Condition** as **greater than**, **Threshold** value as 75 and **Unit** as %

- ° You then need to specify an evaluation window. You have some choices here. The smallest time frame is 5 minutes. This might be a very short time, and you may not want to be alerted if the condition is sustained only for a short period. You need to pick a time frame that meets your requirements. I like alerting, but too much alerting can be noisy and it is very difficult to identify what is really important and needs action, and what is not so important and doesn't need any action from the administrator. If you have an alert set up in this way, you might miss something important if you have more alerts than you can handle. You can configure the time frame to be up to an hour long.

- ° You can specify and action what to do if the report fires. I have specified that you need to e-mail the administrator and co-administrator, and I have also specified that you need to alert someone else, and I have entered my e-mail address.

- ° Ensure that the checkbox called **Enable Rule** is selected, and then click on the tick icon to create the rule:

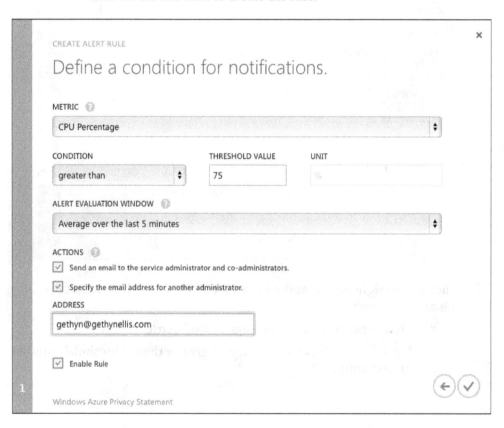

- ° The rule is created and will be visible on the **Management Service** screen:

If your rule fires, you will get an e-mail from Azure, and you can also view the operational log in the Azure portal.

When the alert fires, you will see the alert listed in the **Management Services** pane:

You will also receive an e-mail from Azure telling you that the alert has been fired. You can see this in the following screenshot:

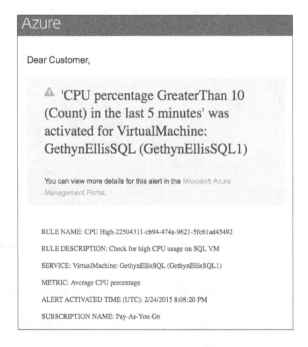

Operational logs

Operational logs in **Management Services** is an interesting feature. The operational logs maintain historical logs of all the create, update, and delete operations that happen on your Azure account. This can be very useful; for example, if you want to find out who disabled a rule on the high CPU usage on your GethynEllisSQL virtual machine. Operational logs let you go back and view 90 days worth of historical data. It will show you which operations have been performed and by whom.

To access the operational logs, you need to perform the following steps:

1. Log in to the Azure Management Portal.
2. From the left-hand side menu, scroll down to the bottom of the list, and click on **Management Services**.

3. Click on the **Operational Logs** menu option in the detail pane. You will see a screen that looks similar to this:

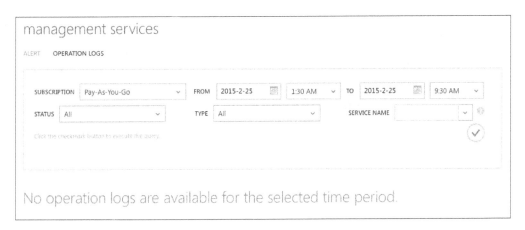

4. Assuming that your log has data in it, you will then need to enter some search criteria. By default, you will get to see the last 8 hours worth of logs. During this time, nothing has happened in the environment. So, I set the date to two days from now, and click on the tick icon to search, and we get a list of logs that are returned:

5. This gives a high-level view of the logs. The one that I have highlighted in the screenshot is the disable rule, where I disabled my CPU high rule to prevent the alert from continuing to fire.

6. You will get some details about the log and the action that it has captured, such as the time when the log was created, whether the event was a success or a failure, who carried out the operation, and so on.

7. To get more information about a particular log, click on the **Detail** button in the footer menu bar, and you will get some additional details in a new window:

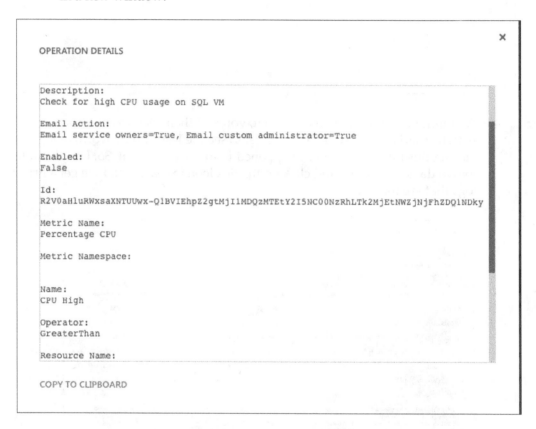

OPERATION DETAILS

```
Description:
Check for high CPU usage on SQL VM

Email Action:
Email service owners=True, Email custom administrator=True

Enabled:
False

Id:
R2V0aHluRWxsaXNTUUwx-Q1BVIEhpZ2gtMjI1MDQzMTEtY2I5NC00NzRhLTk2MjEtNWZjNjFhZDQ1NDky

Metric Name:
Percentage CPU

Metric Namespace:


Name:
CPU High

Operator:
GreaterThan

Resource Name:
```

COPY TO CLIPBOARD

8. There is an option to copy the contents to your clipboard. This will make it easier if you get support from Microsoft on why some resources failed to start. The output reads like this:

```
Culture Code:
en-US
Description:
```

```
Check for high CPU usage on SQL VM
Email Action:
Email service owners=True, Email custom administrator=True
Enabled
False
Id:
R2V0aHluRWxsaXNTUUwx-Q1BVIEhpZ2gtMjI1MDQzMTEtY2I5NC00NzRhLTk2MjEtN
WZjNjFhZDQ1NDky
Metric Name:
Percentage CPU
Metric Namespace:
Name:
CPU High
Operator:
GreaterThan
Resource Name:
GethynEllisSQL1
Resource Type:
virtualmachinesThreshold:
75
WindowSize In Minutes:
5
```

Any failed request that is discovered can easily be tracked down, and if you are engaging Microsoft support, this will help them to help you troubleshoot.

Other monitoring tools

Along with what is available in the Azure portal, you have some other options when it comes to monitoring your cloud-based infrastructure.

PowerShell

We have seen the built-in capabilities for monitoring and alerting that are available through the portal. If you have a large environment, creating the necessary alerts can obviously be time consuming. Wouldn't it be nice to have a way to automate the creation of alerts? Step up PowerShell. PowerShell is Microsoft's scripting tool of choice and can be used to help you create and manage your alerts in Azure.

Keith Meyer has an excellent blog post on this information on the Microsoft TechNet site (`http://blogs.technet.com/b/keithmayer/archive/2014/11/08/scripts-to-tools-automate-monitoring-alert-rules-in-microsoft-azure-with-powershell-and-the-azure-service-management-rest-api.aspx`).

We will use Keith's PowerShell function described here to allow you to create an alert on the CPU percentage for one of our Azure-based virtual machine.

To use Keith's solution, you will need the following:

- The Azure subscription that we created in *Chapter 1, Introduction to Microsoft Azure Cloud Services*

- The Microsoft Azure PowerShell module. This can be downloaded from `http://azure.microsoft.com/en-us/documentation/articles/install-configure-powershell/`

- You will need at least an IaaS virtual machine; we have created several virtual machines with the book so far

- You will need some familiarity with PowerShell

When you have followed the instructions on Keith's blog to set up and create the new PowerShell function in Azure, you can use this function to help you create alerts. The following code can also be used as part of a larger script for the automation of creating alerts.

Then, we can call this function to help you create an alert for our virtual machine:

```
New-AzureAlert '
  -alertName "High CPU" '
  -alertDescription "Higher than 85% CPU utilization" '
  -subscriptionId $subscriptionId '
  -certificate $certificate '
  -cloudServiceName "GethynEllisSQL" '
  -deploymentName "GethynEllisSQL" '
  -roleName "iGethynEllisSQL" '
  -metricName "High CPU" '
  -metricWindowSize "PT30M" '
  -metricOperator "GreaterThan" '
  -metricThreshold 75.00'
  -alertAdmins $true '
  -alertOther gethyn@gethynellis.com
```

This will help us create an alert on high CPU, like the alert we created earlier for the CPU being above 75 percent.

System Center Operation Manager

If you have a large Windows Server estate that you manage and administer, it is likely that you have System Center Operation Manager (SCOM), and this tool is used for monitoring your IT infrastructure.

We will not go into great detail in this book about how to set up and configure SCOM, as this is outside the scope of this book. We will mention what you need to get it working with Azure and provide some SCOM links that can be useful for you to configure SCOM to monitor your cloud-based services.

Install the Windows Azure Management Pack. The management pack can be downloaded from `http://www.microsoft.com/en-us/download/details.aspx?id=38414` and needs to installed on the server running SCOM.

You can obtain management certificates. The communication between SCOM and Azure is secure, and we need to use a certificate. These two links will show you how to create your management certificates:

- `https://msdn.microsoft.com/library/azure/gg551722.aspx`
- `https://msdn.microsoft.com/library/azure/gg432987.aspx`

Add your Azure subscription Operations Manager. Note that you will do this from the **Administration** section of SCOM, and you need to have SCOM 2012 Service Pack 1. You will need the management certificates created earlier.

Import the Azure management packs into SCOM.

With the management packs installed, you can set up Azure monitoring. You can do this using the **Add Monitoring** wizard.

Third-party monitoring tools

There are several third-party products out on the market that can help you monitor your Azure infrastructure. Some of these are open source and available free of charge. You can even get a cloud-based application to do the monitoring for you.

Stackify is available in the Azure market place, and the colleagues that I have spoken to, who have used it, describe this as one of the best tools on the market. The product description says:

> *"Free cloud-based monitoring for web & worker roles, Windows Azure Service Bus Queues, VMs, applications, databases, and more. See all of your application diagnostics and health metrics in one place."*

Others include, but are not limited to the following:

- Quest Cloud Tools
- Opstera: Monitoring for Windows Azure and a scale-out pattern manager

Summary

In this chapter, we looked at how we can set up and collect diagnostic information on our cloud-based virtual machine. We looked at what we need to do to store this information in the cloud, and also how we can integrate monitoring with on-premises tools, such as SCOM. In the next chapter, we will take a look at **Active Directory** in the cloud.

6
Microsoft Azure and Active Directory

In the previous chapters, we built an infrastructure to run Azure-based virtual machines. We looked at how we can create a virtual machine of a variety of types, and how we can network the services together to allow the communication. We also looked at how we can monitor the performance of those virtual machines in the cloud. In this chapter, we will discuss how Active Directory can help you identity and provide access to resources on your IT estate, and how this functionality can be used in the cloud. In this chapter, you will learn the following topics:

- What is Microsoft Azure Active Directory?
- How does **Microsoft Azure Active Directory (WAAD)** work with **Windows Server Active Directory (WSAD)**
- Securing Multi-Factor Authentication
- Managing Microsoft Azure Authentication using PowerShell

What is Microsoft Azure Active Directory?

Active Directory was introduced to the Microsoft stack of technologies way back with Windows Server 2000. It has been around for a long time now. It is used to track and manage resources on your network. It can also be used to provide access to resources on your network. Each new version of Windows Server brings with it some new Active Directory features.

For those who are new to Active Directory, we have included a short section to discuss the Active Directory terminology:

- **Domain**: An Active Directory domain is a collection of objects within your Active Directory network. It can include things such as users, groups of users, and computers.

- **Forest**: This is a collection of domains; if you have a large organization, you may have multiple domains.

- **Organizational Unit (OU)**: This is a container that can be used to group other Active Directory objects together. You can place user groups and computers in organizational units inside your domain. This represents different groups in your business.

- **Groups**: These are Active Directory or local machine objects that can be used to group your users together. They are often used for security and authentication purposes. For example, you might have several file shares that you want only your IT department to have access to. You can create a group called ITGroup, or whatever name best describes your group. Give the group permissions to the necessary file shares, and then simply add every IT user to the group to give them permissions to the three file shares. Thus, you can reduce the administrative overhead of granting each individual user permissions to each file share.

- **Users**: User accounts are what your users will use to log in to your domain and thus are used to authenticate and authorize your users:

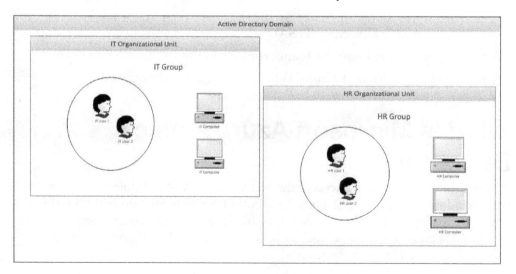

The continued growth of cloud computing and the ability of Microsoft Azure to offer hybrid IT environments allow you to expand your on-premises infrastructure to the cloud. There has been a need to have some form of a directory service in the cloud. This is where Microsoft Azure directory comes into play. It allows you to manage and provide access to your cloud-based resources.

Microsoft Azure Active Directory (Azure AD) is intended to provide you with all your cloud-based access and identity management needs in a simple way. Azure AD works in a similar way to the traditional on-premises Active Directory. Azure AD can be used as a cloud-based directory service, or it can allow you to control the access to all your resources, either in the cloud or on-premises. We will take a look at some of its features in this chapter.

Azure AD editions

Microsoft Azure Active Directory comes in three editions. The edition that you pick will affect how much you pay for Azure AD and which features are available to you. The three editions at the time of writing are as follows:

- **Free**: The free edition of Azure AD allows you to manage your user accounts. You can synchronize your Azure AD with your on-premises Active Directory and have a single sign-on for Azure and Office 365. It can also work with software as a service applications, such as Google Apps and Dropbox. As you can see, the free edition is a pretty comprehensive offering.

- **Basic**: With the basic edition, Azure Active Directory offers application access and self-service identity management requirements. Your users can reset their own passwords. You will get all the capabilities that the free edition has to offer, plus group-based access management, self-service password reset for cloud applications, and Azure Active Directory application proxy (this allows you to publish on-premises web applications using Azure Active Directory). The biggest selling point of the basic edition is the SLA, which states that you will get an uptime of 99.9 percent. If AD is critical to your business needs, and you can't function without it, then MSFT says that it can provide three nines uptime, which equates to just under 9 hours of downtime in a year.

- **Premium**: Premium editions offer all the features of the basic and free edition plus enterprise-level directory services, including Multi-Factor Authentication.

Configuring a standalone Microsoft Azure Active Directory

You get a default Active Directory out of the box when you create an account and subscription in Azure. If you log in to the Azure portal and scroll to the bottom of the left-hand side menu, you will see the **Active Directory** option. If you click on this option, you will see the default directory listed:

Here, you have a number of options that you can select. You can set up your directory, including adding a custom domain and integrating with a local directory, which we will discuss later and try Azure Premium. The other option that we will take a look at here is **Manage Access**:

If you click on **Add domain**, here you can add a domain that your organization owns. To make your user experience more rewarding and user-friendly, they need to know exactly where they are and which organization they are working for. Your organization will need to own the domain though.

Setting up your own domain

The following steps describe how to set up your own domain:

1. Click on the **Add Domain** button.

2. Enter a name for your domain. I am using the name `bigdairandom.com`. Click on the **Next** button.

3. If you plan on integrating with your local Active Directory services to provide your users with a single sign-on experience for Azure, you can check the box. Click on the right arrow:

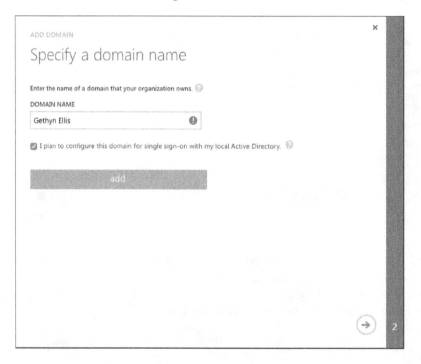

4. The next screen will provide you with the information that your domain registrar will need:

5. You will need to provide your domain registrar with an appropriate record type. Once this has been completed with the domain registrar, you can verify your new domain and complete the process.

Creating a user

To create a user in your Azure-based AD solution you need to sign in to the Azure portal, and navigate to the Active Directory section, using the menu on the left-hand side of the screen. Double-click on the domain that you want to add the user to.

For this example, I am using the default domain:

1. Click on the **Users** option at the top of the menu bar:

2. Click on the **Add User** button at the bottom of the screen. This will start the **Add User** wizard.

3. On the first screen of the wizard, you can choose whether you want to create a new user, add a user with an existing Microsoft account or a user with another Azure AD account. I am going to create a new user in my organization. I will provide a user with the name Seth Ellis, and click on the right arrow to continue:

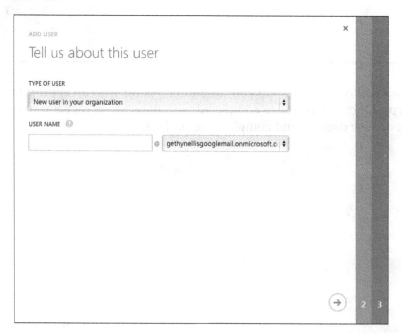

4. On the next screen, you need to provide the user details and add them to any roles you want them to be a member. A role is intended to simplify the security model and access controls. You can think of a role as a way to bundle together a set of access permissions in the form of a role. You can then add users and groups to that role to give them the permissions of that role. The following roles are available:

- **Billing administrator**: As a member of this role, the user can make purchases, manage subscriptions, and monitor the health of services.

- **Global administrator**: This user will have access to all the administrator features. This is given to the user who signs up for the Azure account by default. You must be a member of this role in order to assign other administrator roles.

- **Password administrator**: This user allows the user to reset the password of user.

- **Service administrator**: This user manages the service requests.

- **User administrator**: This user can manage passwords and user accounts.

- **Users**: This user has a standard account for normal users.

In this example, I am going to assign `Seth Ellis` to the user role.

We don't have multifactor configured, but if we want the user to authenticate using Multi-Factor Authentication, we would choose this option. To do this perform the following steps:

1. Enter the correct details, and then click on right arrow:

2. The next screen allows us to generate a temporary password for our user and ensures that they have to change the password when they log in the next time. Click on the **create** button to generate a password:

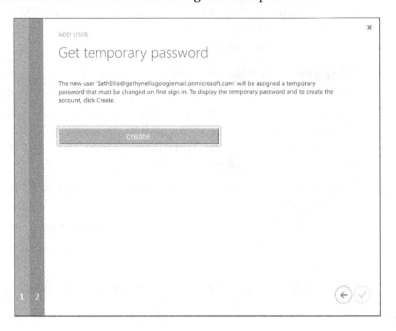

3. You can specify whether to e-mail the password to your user in an e-mail. Note that this will be in a plain text format. Click on the tick icon to create the user:

4. The new user will be added to your directory:

DISPLAY NAME	USER NAME	SOURCED FROM	🔍
Gethyn Ellis →	gethyn.ellis@googlemail.com	Microsoft account	
Seth Ellis	SethEllis@gethynellisgooglemail.onmicrosoft.com	Windows Azure Active Directory	

Creating a group

A group is an object in AD that you can use to group other objects, such as users together, and the group can then be used to give things, such as permissions to your group as a whole. They are intended to simplify and reduce the administration needed. In this section, we will see how we can create a group in our Azure directory.

You need to be logged into the Azure portal. Navigate to the **Active Directory** section in the menu on the left-hand side of the screen.

When you are in the chosen directory, click on the **Groups** menu option from the top menu bar:

Click on the **Add Group** option. This will start the **Add Group** wizard. This is a simple process; give the group a name and a description, and click on the tick icon to create the group:

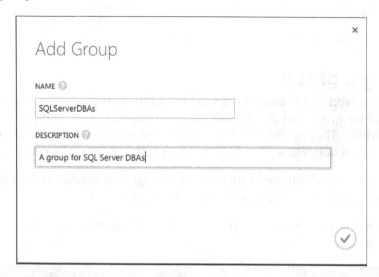

Adding a member to the group

With our group called `SQLServerDBAs` created, we can now make `Seth Ellis` a member of the group.

Double-click on the **SQLServerDBAs** group that we just created. You can see that the group currently has no members:

Click on **Add Members** to start the **Add members** wizard:

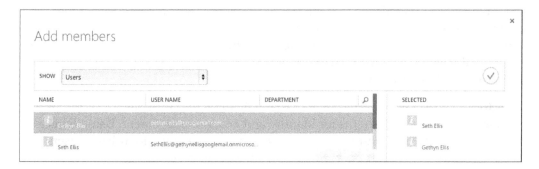

Double-click on each user to add them to the group, and then click on the bottom tick box to add members to the group.

Synchronization of on-premises Active Directory and Azure AD

If you have Active Directory and use it to manage your on-premises network, then it is very likely that, in your move to cloud-based resources, you would want to utilize your established directory of users, groups, and resources. Nobody wants to reinvent the wheel! However, making use of your existing directory will allow you to reduce the time and cost involved in deploying AD to the cloud. It will make this easier for IT administrators, as they will be able to quickly identify with the cloud-based directory and its structure.

In order to do this, you need to make use of Directory Sync. This tool will be a key in integrating your on-premises directory with Azure AD. Directory Sync will allow you to manage your cloud users and groups using your on-premises network. Active Directory management tools allow you to add and remove resources in the cloud, using your on-premises directory.

Directory Sync works on a scheduled basis, so, as you make changes to your on-premises AD, they will be periodically synced with Azure AD. This means that the sync doesn't happen in real time, so if you make a mistake, depending on your timings, it's not instantly added to the cloud.

There are three types of Directory Sync:

Directory Sync

We have already established that for many companies, who already have a mature on-premises Active Directory environment setup and configured the ability to utilize the work that has already been completed on setting up and configuring, this would be of great benefit, as they move to the cloud. They want to be able to take their user accounts and AD groups to the cloud.

Directory Sync is a very important tool that will allow you to achieve this and uses your existing users and groups for identity and access management. Using Directory Sync, you can use your on-premises AD tools to manage your cloud-based users and groups. In fact, using your on-premises AD tools, you can create and remove users and groups from your cloud-based AD environment.

This works on a scheduled basis and the changes made to your AD on-premises environment will get synced to the cloud on schedule. This lack of real-time sync can be beneficial; it can allow you to rectify any issues or mistakes before they get replicated to the cloud. Notice that passwords are not synced, and your users and groups based in the cloud will need to activate this, with users being sent different usernames and passwords.

Directory Sync with password

The ability to sync passwords extends to Directory Sync. You can still manage your cloud-based users and groups. When password sync is enabled on the Directory Sync computer, your end users will be able to use the same password that they use when logging into your on-premises AD environment for their cloud-based services, such as Office 365. Dynamics CRM Password Sync is an extension to the Directory Sync Scenario.

The process of password synchronization involves the extraction of your user password hash from the on-premises AD. Additional security processing is applied to the password hash before it is synchronized with AD. This is to reassure you that your password is safe and secure as it synchronizes with the cloud.

The Azure website says that plain text versions of the user password are not exposed to the sync tool and Azure AD and its associated services. So, in fact, the plain text version of your password doesn't leave your on-premises environment, so in theory, it can't be intercepted.

Again, the benefits of password sync solutions are that they reduce the AD management costs and simplify your user experience.

Directory Sync with single sign-on

Directory Sync with single sign-on, which is also known as an identity federation, is the most complete solution for integrating your on-premises Active Directory with the cloud. This solution should provide your users with the most seamless integration of on-premises and cloud-based directory services for identity and access management.

Without single sign-on, your users would need to maintain separate usernames and passwords for your online and on-premises accounts. To make use of single sign-on, you will need both Directory Sync and **security token service (STS)**.

A security token service enables Directory Sync with single sign-on. This extends the notion of centralized authentication to web applications and services located anywhere. When you configure STS to provide single sign-on to Azure, you will be creating a federated trust between your on-premises STS and the federated domain you've specified in Azure.

Azure AD supports single sign-on scenarios that use either of the following security token services:

- **Active Directory Federation Services (ADFS)**
- Shibboleth identity provider
- Third-party identity providers

Multi-Factor Authentication

Multi-Factor Authentication can be set up and configured to be used to provide multifactor capabilities to all of your cloud applications and services that are based in Azure. Using a variety of authentication options, you can secure Microsoft and the third-party applications hosted in Azure. The long and short of this process is that your user can provide their username and password, which is submitted to Azure. The user is then left with a challenge to interact with some other devices to complete the authentication. It is only when this process is complete that the user is provided access to the service. This means that your user will need both their username and password combination along with access to the device specified that will confirm their identity, adding an extra level of security to the authentication process.

Summary

In this chapter, we discussed the options that were available to you when it came to making use of Microsoft Azure Directory Services. We looked at how we can create a cloud-based directory and discussed the options available for integrating your on-premises Active Directory with the cloud in order to allow you to integrate your on-premises Active Directory seamlessly to manage your cloud-based resources. In the next chapter, we will discuss high availability and disaster recovery.

7

High Availability and Disaster Recovery for Azure Virtual Machines

In this chapter, we will take a look at how we can configure our virtual machines for High Availability and ensure that we are protected in the event of a disaster. You might think that **High Availability (HA)** and **Disaster Recovery (DR)** are built into your cloud solution. Well, only if you configure your environment in this way. If you don't, and Azure data center has a proverbial hiccup, then your systems will go down and will be unavailable. Though Azure is fully customizable, you can benefit from its flexibility by protecting your on-site servers from a disaster by allowing the Azure cloud to be your Disaster Recovery solution.

In this chapter, you will learn the following topics:

- Microsoft Azure High Availability
- Creating an Availability Set
- Creating and configuring a Traffic Manager profile

Microsoft Azure High Availability

To make any cloud solution that you design for your applications highly available, you need to design and implement a strategy that allows you to absorb any outage to your cloud provider. In effect, we want our application/functionality to be available to our users/customers despite a failure in the cloud platform.

The driver behind High Availability is the business need and the cost of an outage to key applications or services to the business. In particular, the outage prevents the business from generating revenue or costing the business in terms of opportunity cost or opportunity lost. Thus, businesses generally place great importance on their mission-critical applications and are generally prepared to invest capital to ensure that they remain available. The importance of the business places in an application will dictate how important the application's availability is to the business. This is true regardless of the platform the application is running on. Whether it is one of the many cloud providers, on-premises physical infrastructure, or your own private cloud/virtual platform. It is important to consider the business needs. While availability is important, we don't want to introduce unnecessary complexity and cost to our high-available design, when in fact, there was no need for such complexity in the first place.

Consider someone who travels for work as an analogy for high availability. You pack all you need for a week on the road, living out of your suitcase from a hotel room. You wear a pair of trousers and pack five clean shirts. While you are out for dinner on Tuesday evening, you spill red wine on your trousers and shirt. You have a spare shirt, but you only have one pair of trousers. Now, you can still wear your trousers covered in red wine while you go and buy a new pair from the shop. You will endure the embarrassment of having red wine spilt on you, but you might not want the red wine look while you are in the office. A workaround to this and to avoid the inconvenience of having to go shopping, you could have packed an additional pair of trousers. This extra pair of trousers may remain redundant and be never used, but you have them in case you need them. If you have a cloud service that is designed to copy in such a situation where you have lost some capabilities, you'll be in a situation whereby some relatively minor problems don't bring down your entire application. It might be that it continues to run, maybe with a degradation in the performance. Or you can build in your redundancy upfront to prevent against the performance hit in the event of an issue.

There are a few traits that you would expect a highly available cloud offering to provide:

- System availability
- System scalability
- Redundancy and fault tolerance

These characteristics are related to each other. However, it is important to understand each individually, how they relate, and how they contribute to the overall availability of the final solution that we design for our systems and applications.

System availability

When we take a look at the availability of a service, we will need to take a look at the infrastructure supporting it and any dependent services that need to be available for your service to be available. Consider a shopping cart on an e-commerce site. You might have your shopping cart set up and available, but you may use a third-party solution for the payment. When your customer checks out, they will need the third-party payment solution to be available for their orders to be completed. If your shopping cart is available but the payment gateway is not, your application is not fully available. So, there is a dependency on the payment gateway for our solution to be available.

When we design a highly available application, we want to try and remove any single points of failure. This can be achieved through building redundancy and resilience in to the design. When designing a highly available solution in Microsoft Azure, we need to consider the availability of the platform and its components and how each of them can have an impact on the availability of our system. Microsoft uses a term called effective availability to describe this.

Effective availability considers each dependant component and the **service level agreement (SLA)** for that component. The cumulative effect of each service component is then considered when we take a look at the total system availability. When it comes to designing our systems and analyzing the potential outage potential, we would take a look at the SLA of each component we have used, the SLA that Microsoft has for that component, and then take a look at how the sum of all these small things helps you decide the potential impact on the availability of our system.

System availability is often measured in 9s as a percentage of system availability time. If we say that a system has an SLA of three nines that is 99.9 percent uptime, this equates to just under nine hours of downtime a year. Microsoft System availability is measured by the percentage of a given time window the system will be able to operate.

System scalability

Scalability will have a direct effect on availability — for example; who has tried to buy tickets for a music concert or sporting event and the website times out or crashes as the systems creeks and breaks due to the demand for the tickets and load on the servers? If we have an application that fails because of the load being applied by the end users, then it is no longer available. If we envisage the load expanding and contracting on our servers, then we should design a solution that can scale as the user base grows. Thus, we should be able to satisfy our customers and clients and maintain the availability of our application.

When we talk about a system being scalable, we usually suggest scaling up or scaling out. Scaling up is sometimes called scaling vertically, while scaling out can be referred to as horizontal scaling. Scaling out means adding more machines or servers to help the server with our workload. The machines are likely to be of similar specifications to our existing machines. Scaling up or vertical scaling means increasing the capacity of the existing servers and machines, adding more CPU and memory, and so on. With virtual machines that reside in Azure, it's easier to scale horizontally, that is, add more machines to service an application than it is to change the capacity of the existing VMs. Scaling up will mean a redeployment or the virtual machine that is not really practical and probably involves downtime. Cost is another thing to consider; if you scale out, you can generally stay on the same pricing model, albeit paying for additional resources at that level. Scaling up means changing your machine to a different pricing tier. If the cost is important to you, this also needs to be evaluated when making a decision to scale your cloud-based system.

Redundancy and fault tolerance

Physical IT hardware has a failure rate and applications need to be designed, keeping this in mind. This is not a new fact for an IT professional to deal with if you were to ask any IT professional, who has been in the industry for several years or before the popularity of cloud-based solutions. Many of the systems built and designed on-premises using physical servers would have had some elements of redundancy built in to them so that the system can cope with a hardware failure. Examples include, but are not limited to RAID Arrays for local storage so that the storage can cope with a disk failure; **Storage Area Networks (SAN)** have built-in redundancy to cope with disk failures, multiple power supplies, and multiple network cards. All physical design implementations that are intended to prevent an outage in the event of a failure are one of these components.

There is no difference when it comes designing solutions for Microsoft Azure. With the cloud, we don't have control over the physical implementation of the hardware. We have to assume that, at some point, one of the components used in our cloud solution will fail or be unavailable. In Azure's short history, we have seen examples of outages in certain services. Using the SLAs and features offered by Microsoft Azure, we need to design our cloud-based system to be able to keep functioning in the event of such a failure.

Azure virtual machine downtime and availability

There are two types of downtime that can impact the availability of Azure virtual machine, and we should consider both planned and unplanned downtime, when discussing virtual machine availability:

- **Planned**: Microsoft will advise planned downtime. These events happen from time to time as a result of updates made by Microsoft to the underlying Azure platform. There could be a variety of different reasons but would normally involve some changes being made to the underlying infrastructure that the virtual machine is running on. These events don't necessarily mean an outage to the virtual machine; it's possible that the changes will have no impact on the uptime of your virtual machine. However, if a situation arises whereby the changes made require a restart or reboot of the virtual machine, then you are still going to get an outage for that virtual machine. Whether that impacts your application availability will depend on your Azure virtual machine infrastructure design.

- **Unplanned**: This is an unexpected outage. You will not receive a notification in advance informing or warning you of the downtime. To maintain availability during such a downtime or outage, you need an appropriate application design that minimizes the impact of the outage.

These unplanned outages are likely to occur when the underlying physical infrastructure that your virtual machine is running on has failed or faulted. The types of failures that you can encounter will vary, but they are similar to the issues that you could face when you run into issues running an on-premises virtual environment. Some common issues are listed, but note that this is not an exclusive list:

- Disk drive failure
- Power failures
- Network issues

If Azure detects these failures, then it will migrate your virtual machine from the failed host it is currently running on to a host that is functioning correctly and has the capacity to run the virtual machine. For those of you who are familiar with on-premises virtualization technology, this is similar to making a virtual machine highly available, and Hyper-V or ESX will restart the machine on a healthy physical host. Such events are rare, but depending on the nature of the physical hardware, failure may also cause your virtual machine to reboot during this process.

The multiple-tier architecture

Before we move on and take a look at how we can implement highly available virtual machines that are protected in the event of a disaster in the Microsoft Azure cloud, we need to briefly discuss the application design and tiers that are found in typical application designs. Most systems and applications are divided into multiple tiers with each tier performing a different role in the system. These tiers allow you to deliver an available, scalable, fault-tolerant system to your business. As we've discussed, this is the objective of any highly available system, including cloud-based ones. Here, I'm going to look at the three basic tiers of simple web applications, which are as follows:

- **Client tier**: Sometimes, this tier is called the presentation tier. This usually contains the user interface; in our case, this might be a client device and browser.

- **Application tier**: Sometimes, this is called the logic tier and carries out the application logic and business processing. In our case, this would be our web server running the web application.

- **Data tier**: This is where the data of the application is stored and persisted to disk. For the purposes of our example, this would be a database server, such as a SQL Server.

In the following architecture diagram, we have an example of a system architecture separated by the various tiers for a web application. Assume that it is currently an on-premises system:

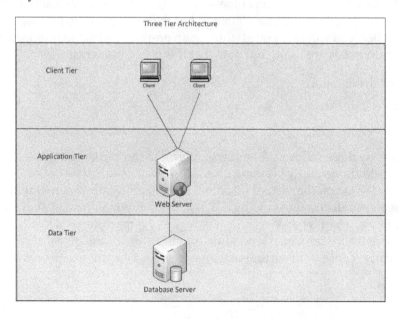

It is worth noting here that, although this is using a three-tier architecture, there are several single points of failure that can cause an outage. For example, if we lose either the web server or the database server in this setup, we would lose the system all together. If the web server comes under a load from clients that it can't support, then some of our users are likely to get timeout errors.

Therefore, this is not the high availability that we desire. As this system has been designed using the multi-tier approach, we can add redundancy to the various tiers to build our fault tolerance, scalability, and availability, we should get a failure somewhere in the stack, or we need to improve the capacity of the system:

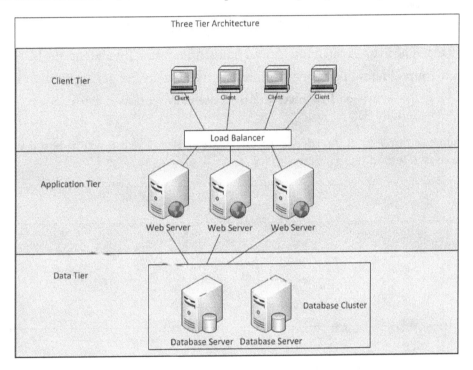

In the preceding architecture diagram, we have added multiple web servers to the application tier, and we have added a load balancer to distribute the workload, hopefully, evenly among the web servers. If we lose a web server, our application will be able to continue to function, as we'll have two other servers processing the logic. In the data tier, we have implemented SQL Server clustering, which means that if the database server nodes fail, there is another node available to satisfy the requests for the data. We have got availability, scalability, and fault tolerance built in to the system.

How do we implement such a design when working with the Microsoft Azure cloud? Microsoft understands that availability, scalability, and fault tolerance are important to their clients and the businesses they support, so they have provided something called an Availability Set. By creating an Availability Set and adding virtual machines to the Availability Set, Azure will ensure that the virtual machines in the set get distributed across the physical hosts that run them in such a way that a hardware failure will not bring down all the machines in the set.

Microsoft has some recommendations and requirements when it comes to using Availability Sets. These are as follows:

- Ensure that your Availability Set has multiple virtual machines.
  It is important to avoid a situation where you have a single virtual machine in an Availability Set, as this configuration invalidates the SLA.

- Group different tiers together into one Availability Set per application tier.

- Use the Azure load balancer to distribute your workload across your Availability Set.

If we wish to implement the preceding application design using Azure-based virtual machines, we would have a diagram like this:

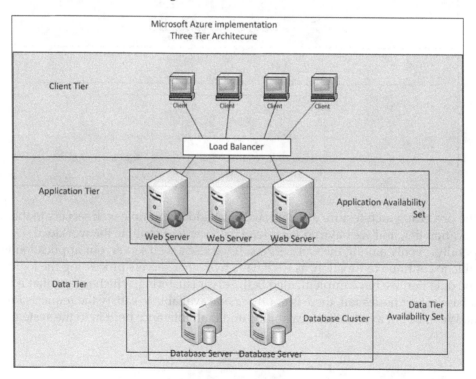

The cloud-based deployment of our initial application has created two Availability Sets. One for the application/logic tier and one for the data tier. This will ensure that the machines in each tier are distributed in such a way that, in the event of a an outage, either planned or unplanned on a given underlying host in Azure, not all virtual machines in the application tier will be affected at the same time. Thus, the outage does not take down the entire application and the system will remain available, albeit with a reduced capacity. We have created multiple virtual machines, so we meet the Microsoft SLA agreement. This means we can get 99.95 percent uptime for our virtual machines. This equates to just over four and half hours a year of downtime.

Another benefit of grouping our servers by Availability Sets is the ability to scale the application. Our application is a web application. It's a web application for a ticket reseller. They know that the tickets for the latest and greatest Boy Band Tour will be going on sale in the next week or so. The benefit of Azure is that they can quickly add additional computing resources in the form of application servers to cope with the extra demand and then remove them again when the demand passes.

Azure has its own load balancer called Traffic Manager. It is located in the **Traffic Manager** section of the Azure portal. By combining Availability Sets and the Azure load balancer, you can build a resilient application. Traffic Manager has the ability to monitor your virtual machines, and if an issue is detected automatically, it stops directing the traffic there. It would work as follows; the Azure Load Balancer distributes traffic between the different virtual machines that you specify in your traffic manager profile; you can choose the distribution used. Traffic Manager distributes traffic to your virtual machines; if an issue is detected through the monitoring of Traffic Manager, it would automatically stop directing traffic to the affected virtual machines. It is worth noting here that the load balancer is included in the standard tier virtual machines, as our basic tier virtual machines would not have the load balancer included.

If you do not configure the load balancer to send traffic to multiple virtual machines, then a maintenance event that affects the virtual machines that serve traffic potentially, causing an outage for some of your users. Making use of the load balancer and placing multiple virtual machines that reside in the same application tier under the same load balancer and Availability Set will mean that traffic and hence, your users will be continuously served by at least one virtual machine.

Hopefully, you can see why Microsoft also recommends not having a single virtual machine in an availability group. It would be impossible for them to adhere to the 99.95 percent SLA with only one machine in the availability group. You will, in fact, get a warning from the management portal if you try to create an Availability Set with a single virtual machine in it:

> **ⓘ** IMPORTANT   The availability set for this virtual machine has only one running instance, which affects the service level agreement (SLA). The SLA requires at least two running virtual machine instances. Learn more

Availability Set – Azure Internals

There are some internal processes to make you aware of when you can configure multiple virtual machines in an Availability Set. This will be transparent to the end user, but it is worth being aware of the internals so that you can establish how many VMs will be potentially unavailable to you in the event of a planned reboot. Azure will do the following to each VM in the set:

- Allocate an **Update Domain (UD)**
- Allocate a **Fault Domain (FD)**

An Update Domain is used to determine the sets of virtual machines and the underlying hardware that can be rebooted together. For each Availability Set created, five UDs will be created. When virtual machines are added to an Availability Set, they are allocated a UD. If we had allocated five VMs to an Availability Set, they would have been allocated to each of the UDs. When we add a sixth virtual machine, this VM will be allocated to the same UD as the first, and so on in a round-robin basis. The UD numbers are not used to determine the reboot order, so UD 5 would be rebooted before UD 1.

The following diagram shows the five UDs in an Availability Set and how the VMs get allocated to a UD as they are added to the Availability Set. Note that when the sixth VM is added, it is added to the same UD as the first:

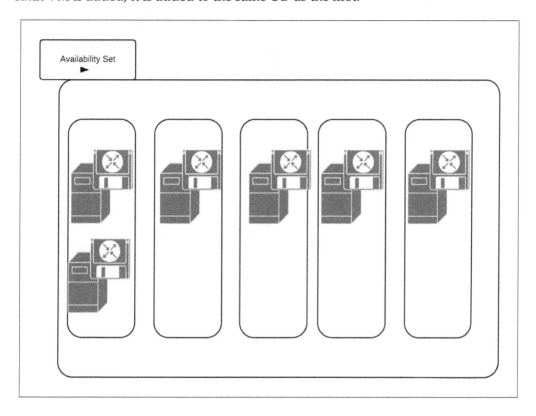

In the event of a planned outage that requires a reboot of UD1, we would potentially lose two of the virtual machines for the period of the reboot.

Fault Domains (FD) are also allocated to virtual machines as they are added to an Availability Set. Fault domains are used to define the group of virtual machines of physical resources, such as networking and power. Availability Sets will, by default, be separated by two FDs.

These two internal structures ensure that, by placing your VMs into an Availability Set, you will be protected in the event of physical hardware failures or power interruptions. In the following diagram, we have an Availability Set that has been allocated three virtual machines that have been placed in one of the two FDs for the Availability Set. This means that two of the three VMs share resources, such as power and networking. If the hardware that supports the FD with the VMs in it fails, we have another VM running, using a different set of resources, negating the application downtime of the unexpected interruption:

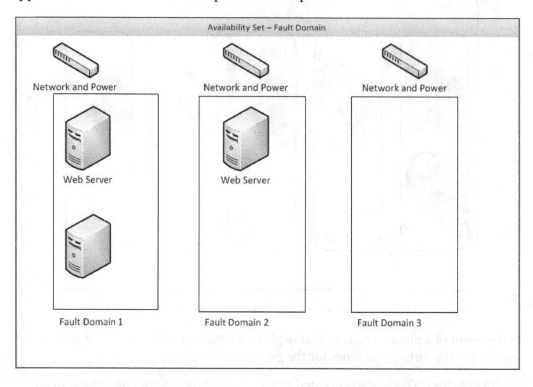

Put simply, Update Domains are used for planned maintenance events, such as Azure upgrades or patches by Microsoft, ensuring that not all the VMs that, support a tier in your architecture are rebooted at the same time. Fault Domains ensure that in the event of an unplanned hardware failure, the virtual machines in your application tier are not all affected by the underlying hardware failure.

Configuring an Availability Set

When it comes to configuring an Availability Set for your virtual machines, you have two options. You can configure the Availability Set when you create the virtual machine, or you can change an existing virtual machine and add it to an Availability Set. We will discuss both here.

Creating an Availability Set when provisioning a virtual machine

You can create an Availability Set when you provision a virtual machine. This will create a new virtual machine and make it part of a new Availability Set:

1. Log in to the Azure portal using your credentials.

2. Follow the process to create a virtual machine. We took at look at this in more detail in *Chapter 2, Creating and Deploying a Windows Virtual Machine* and *Chapter 3, Deploying Linux Virtual Machines on Azure*.

3. On page number 3 of the **Virtual machine configuration** wizard, you will be prompted if you would like to add the machine to an **Availability Set**. Change the option to **Create an availability set**.

4. Give the **Availability Set** a name. I have named mine TESTAS:

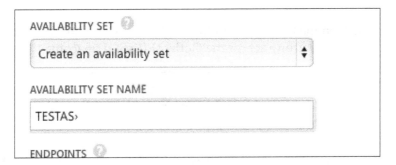

5. Complete the **Virtual machine configuration** wizard, and you will be able to create a new VM and an Availability Set.

Creating a new Availability Set for an existing virtual machine

You can add an existing virtual machine to an existing Availability Set, or you can create a new Availability Set for an existing virtual machine. In this section, we will run through the process of creating an Availability Set and adding a group, and then we will take a look at adding a virtual machine to an Availability Set that already exists:

1. Log in to the portal using your credentials.

2. Navigate to the **Virtual Machine** option on the left-hand side of the menu.

3. Click on the virtual machine you want to add to an availability group:

4. Then, click on the **Configure** option. In this example, I am going to create a new availability group set for the **GethynEllisSQL** machine:

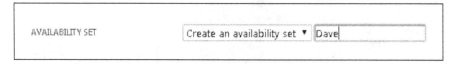

5. In the settings option, you have a section for the Availability Set. In the **Availability Set** drop-down list, ensure that an Availability Set is created.

6. Give the Availability Set a name. In this case, I have named mine `Dave`.

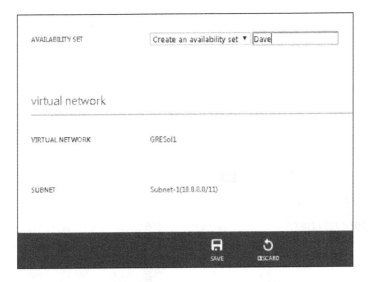

7. Click on the **Save** option to create the Availability Set, and add the virtual machine to it.

For the Availability Set to be considered for the Microsoft SLA, it needs to have at least two virtual machines in the availability group. Now we have created a group, we can add additional virtual machines to it.

1. To do this, in the **Virtual Machine** section of the portal, click on the virtual machine you want to add to the Availability Set.

2. Click on the **Configure** tab.

3. In the **Availability Set** section, choose the group you wish to add it to; in this case, I will choose **Dave**:

4. Click on the **Save** button at the bottom of the screen to add the virtual machine to the **Availability Set**.

5. You can remove a virtual machine from an **Availability Set** too; in the availability group section of the virtual machine, just choose the **Remove from availability set** option and click on **Save**:

The Microsoft Azure load balancer and Availability Set

Microsoft Azure has its own load balancer. The Azure Traffic Manager allows you to control the distribution of the user traffic. The Azure Traffic Manager has three load balancing methods available to help you distribute traffic:

*   **Failover**: This is used when you want to offer a backup service. If this primary service fails or becomes unavailable, client requests will get redirected to a backup.

*   **Performance**: Performance load balancing is used if you have services that span more than one geographic region, and you want to direct your users to the closest geographic region. This can reduce network latency. If you want traffic that comes from the USA to be directed to US-based virtual machine and European users to be directed to European-based virtual machine this is the method to use.

*   **Round Robin**: This is one of the most common options used in load balancers. Traffic is distributed to each VM in turn. You can use this method when you want to distribute loads across a set of cloud services in the same data center or across cloud services or websites in different data centers. This is what we will use in our configuration.

To create a Traffic Management Profile in Azure, you need to perform the following steps:

1. Log in to the portal using the credentials that you created in *Chapter 1, Introduction to Microsoft Azure Cloud Services.*

2. On the left-hand side menu, scroll down to the **Traffic Manager** option:

3. Click on **Create a New Traffic Manager Profile** option:

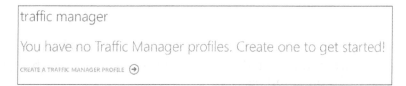

4. The next screen that appears is the **Create Traffic Manager profile** wizard. Give your traffic manager profile a DNS prefix. This will be what you will point your clients to. I have named mine WebRRSales, and then decide on the load balancing method. I will choose **Round Robin** and click on **Create**:

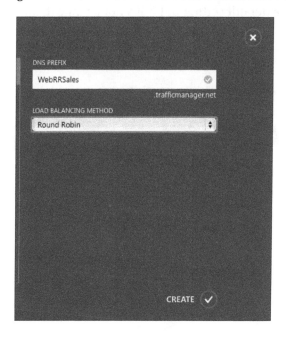

5. When the profile has been created, this may take a minute or two, the next step is to configure the endpoints to use. This will be the virtual machine we want to load balance.

6. On the **Traffic Manager** screen, in the management portal, the profile that we created should be listed. Double-click on the profile, and then click on the **Endpoints** tab. Then, click on the **Add Endpoints** option:

7. The **Service Type** drop-down list has two options: **Cloud Services** and **Web App**. **Cloud Services** should be the default setting. If it's not, change the drop-down list to **Cloud Services**.

8. Select the virtual machines that you want to send traffic to in a load balanced way. In this case, this would be the virtual machines that act as a web server.

9. Click on the tick icon to add the endpoints to the profile.

10. Finally, click on the **Configure** tab to ensure that **Round Robin** is selected. It should be the default setting but if it's not change it, and then click on **Save**:

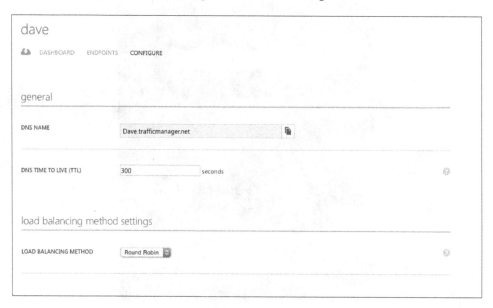

The last step would be to point our client applications to the traffic manager endpoint, and it will start to distribute load-balanced traffic to the virtual machines in the Traffic Manager Profile.

Microsoft Azure as a Disaster Recovery site

Late in 2014, Microsoft announced that it was introducing Azure site recovery. In effect, this is Microsoft's version of Disaster Recovery as a service. The Microsoft Cloud will act as your Disaster Recovery site. This potentially means that you don't need to maintain multiple sites for the purposes of on-premises Disaster Recovery. You have your main on-premises site, which you would replicate to Azure.

There are other providers out there too, such as VMware's vCloud Air Disaster Recovery. The choice really comes down to what virtualization technology you are using on-premises. We will briefly discuss Microsoft's Azure Disaster recovery site solution—Azure site recovery. It's relatively self-explanatory; it lets you replicate the Hyper-V machines running on your premises into Azure. You can then use these replicated machines for Disaster Recovery with minimal additional work.

Configuring and setting up site recovery is outside the scope of this book. However, there are a numbers of benefits listed in the next section, and, if you are working in a hybrid environment, you can make use of Microsoft Azure to help you build a Disaster Recovery environment without the need of your own physical location. For more information on this, visit `http://azure.microsoft.com/en-gb/documentation/articles/hyper-v-recovery-manager-overview/`.

Summary

In this chapter, we looked at the high availability options that you have when configuring virtual machines in Azure. You have a number of options available to you, when configuring both your Azure-based VMs to be highly available, including the ability to create Availability Sets. You can make use of Azure site recovery to use the Azure cloud as a Disaster Recovery site for both your cloud-based virtual machines and your on-premises Hyper-V virtual machines.

Index

U

Ubuntu 46
Update Domain (UD) 134

V

virtualization 3-5
virtual machine
  creating, gallery used 25-28
  pricing 22-24
  redeploying, into virtual network 71-76
virtual network configurations
  cloud-only virtual network 63, 64
  cross-premises virtual network 65-67
virtual networks
  benefits 62, 63
  configuring 67
virtual network topology 63

W

Windows server virtual machine
  additional data disks, adding to 35-40
  connecting 29
  connecting, from RDP 31, 32
  connecting, in portal 31
  creating 17-21
  managing 29
  pricing, for virtual machines 22-24
  starting 29, 30
  stopping 29, 30
  working, with PowerShell 33-35

Thank you for buying
Microsoft Azure IaaS Essentials

About Packt Publishing

Packt, pronounced 'packed', published its first book, *Mastering phpMyAdmin for Effective MySQL Management*, in April 2004, and subsequently continued to specialize in publishing highly focused books on specific technologies and solutions.

Our books and publications share the experiences of your fellow IT professionals in adapting and customizing today's systems, applications, and frameworks. Our solution-based books give you the knowledge and power to customize the software and technologies you're using to get the job done. Packt books are more specific and less general than the IT books you have seen in the past. Our unique business model allows us to bring you more focused information, giving you more of what you need to know, and less of what you don't.

Packt is a modern yet unique publishing company that focuses on producing quality, cutting-edge books for communities of developers, administrators, and newbies alike. For more information, please visit our website at www.packtpub.com.

About Packt Enterprise

In 2010, Packt launched two new brands, Packt Enterprise and Packt Open Source, in order to continue its focus on specialization. This book is part of the Packt Enterprise brand, home to books published on enterprise software – software created by major vendors, including (but not limited to) IBM, Microsoft, and Oracle, often for use in other corporations. Its titles will offer information relevant to a range of users of this software, including administrators, developers, architects, and end users.

Writing for Packt

We welcome all inquiries from people who are interested in authoring. Book proposals should be sent to author@packtpub.com. If your book idea is still at an early stage and you would like to discuss it first before writing a formal book proposal, then please contact us; one of our commissioning editors will get in touch with you.

We're not just looking for published authors; if you have strong technical skills but no writing experience, our experienced editors can help you develop a writing career, or simply get some additional reward for your expertise.

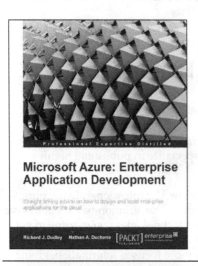

**Microsoft Azure: Enterprise
Application Development**

ISBN: 978-1-84968-098-1   Paperback: 248 pages

Straight talking advice on how to design and build
enterprise applications for the cloud

1. Build scalable enterprise applications using
    Microsoft Azure.

2. The perfect fast-paced case study for
    developers and architects wanting to enhance
    core business processes.

3. Packed with examples to illustrate concepts.

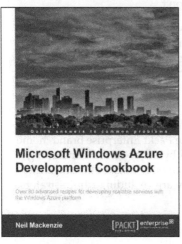

**Microsoft Windows Azure
Development Cookbook**

ISBN: 978-1-84968-222-0   Paperback: 392 pages

Over 80 advanced recipes for developing scalable
services with the Windows Azure platform

1. Packed with practical, hands-on cookbook
    recipes for building advanced, scalable cloud-
    based services on the Windows Azure platform
    explained in detail to maximize your learning.

2. Extensive code samples showing how to use
    advanced features of Windows Azure blobs,
    tables and queues.

3. Understand remote management of Azure
    services using the Windows Azure Service
    Management REST API.

Please check **www.PacktPub.com** for information on our titles

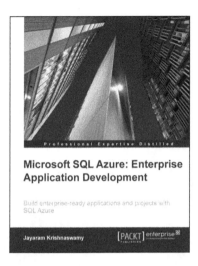

Microsoft SQL Azure: Enterprise
Application Development

Build enterprise-ready applications and projects with
SQL Azure

Jayaram Krishnaswamy

Microsoft SQL Azure Enterprise Application Development

ISBN: 978-1-84968-080-6   Paperback: 420 pages

Build enterprise-ready applications and projects
with SQL Azure

1. Develop large scale enterprise applications
   using Microsoft SQL Azure.

2. Understand how to use the various third
   party programs such as DB Artisan, RedGate,
   ToadSoft etc developed for SQL Azure.

3. Master the exhaustive Data migration and
   Data Synchronization aspects of SQL Azure.

Windows Azure Programming
Patterns for Start-ups

A step-by-step guide to create easy solutions to build your
business using Windows Azure services

Riccardo Becker

Windows Azure programming patterns for Start-ups

ISBN: 978-1-84968-560-3   Paperback: 292 pages

A step-by-step guide to create easy solutions to build
your business using Windows Azure services

1. Explore the different features of Windows
   Azure and its unique concepts.

2. Get to know the Windows Azure platform by
   code snippets and samples by a single start-up
   scenario throughout the whole book.

3. A clean example scenario demonstrates the
   different Windows Azure features.

Please check **www.PacktPub.com** for information on our titles

www.ingramcontent.com/pod-product-compliance
Lightning Source LLC
Chambersburg PA
CBHW060137060326
40690CB00018B/3919